KING of GLORY

ILLUSTRATED STUDY GUIDE

A COMPANION TOOL FOR THE KING OF GLORY MOVIE & BOOK

REINFORCING THE STORY & MESSAGE

KING OF GLORY ILLUSTRATED STUDY GUIDE

Copyright © 2018, 2023 ROCK International. All rights reserved.

ISBN 978-1-62041-005-9

A Publication of ROCK International
Relief, **O**pportunity & **C**are for **K**ids • www.rockintl.org
Resources **O**f **C**rucial **K**nowledge • www.rockintl.org/resources
P.O. Box 4766, Greenville, SC 29608 • resources@rockintl.org
www.king-of-glory.com

P. D. Bramsen, writer and graphic editor
J. Hodgins, graphic designer and writer
Artwork taken from the KING of GLORY book & movie
Arminda San Martín, primary illustrator
Cole Phail, secondary illustrator
Andrew Harmon, contributing artist
Special thanks to the many who field-tested and proofed this study guide.

Photo credits
Photos with Creative Commons (CC) license are from https://commons.wikimedia.org

Page 3	Hubble Telescope image of RS Puppis, a Cepheid variable star, NASA, public domain
Page 7	KING of GLORY Garage Studio, South Carolina, August 2013, Cole Phail
Pages 14-15	Infrared image of a small part of the Milky Way galaxy, NASA
Page 21	A beautiful Dawn in Tarkarli by Striker2002, CC 4.0
Page 25	Earthrise, NASA
Page 33	Earth/Moon/Sun, NASA Goddard Space Flight Center/Scientific Visualization Studio
Page 59	Bryce Canyon: a giant natural amphitheater created by erosion, Luca Galuzzi, CC 2.5
Page 84	Gospel of Matthew Papyrus, University of Michigan, Public Domain
Page 84	Papyrus plants, SuSanA Secretariat, CC 2.0
Page 88	Bethlehem Countryside, James Emery, CC 2.0
Page 93	Jordan River, David Bjorgen, CC 2.5
Page 99	Magellanic Cloud (one of the Milky Way's closest galactic neighbors), NASA
Page 133	Heel bone with nail, Israel Museum. Photographer: Ilan Shtulman
Page 145	Ancient Philippi, Mrpany Goff, CC 3.0
Pages 65, 73, 119, 121, 123, 138-139	Middle East, P. D. Bramsen, 2004

Unless otherwise marked, Scripture quotations used in this book are taken from
the Holy Bible, *The New International Version* © 1995 Zondervan Corporation.
Scripture quotations marked NLT are taken from the Holy Bible, *New Living Translation*,
Copyright © 1996, 2004, 2007. Used by permission of Tyndale House Publishers, Inc.
All rights reserved. These Scripture versions are chosen for their simple English
in order to make the story and message understandable to all, including those
for whom English is not their first language.

To read or watch or freely download KING of GLORY in dozens of other languages,
please visit **www.king-of-glory.com**

To translate and produce the KING of GLORY movie, book, this study guide,
or any of ROCK's resources into other languages, please write to:
resources@rockintl.org

Hubble Telescope image on right: This bright pulsating star (named *RS Puppis* by astronomers),
shrouded by dark, thick clouds of gas and dust, is just one of more than 100 billion stars
in the Milky Way galaxy in which earth, its sun, moon, and other planets are located.
RS Puppis is over ten times bigger and about 15,000 times brighter than our sun.

Printed in the USA

KING OF GLORY
FROM THE FIRST EPISODE

Would you like to meet the One who formed you?
Would you like to live forever with the Maker
and Master of the galaxies? You can.
He has revealed Himself. He wants you to know Him.
He wants your family and community
to know Him too. He invites you
to understand His plan, experience His love,
behold His majesty, submit to His rule,
and live for His glory. But He will not force you
to be His subject. After all, He is not just *a* king.
He is *the* King. *The King of glory.*

This is His story.

EPISODE SELECTION

PART 1: THE KING FORETELLS HIS PLAN
— Old Testament —

PART 2: THE KING FULFILLS HIS PLAN
— New Testament —

SPECIAL FEATURES

WATCH the MOVIE in your language now:
www.king-of-glory.com

KNOWING YOUR TOOLS

I keep six honest serving-men
(They taught me all I knew);
Their names are **What** and **Why** and **When**
And **How** and **Where** and **Who**.

— RUDYARD KIPLING, 1865-1936, AUTHOR OF *THE JUNGLE BOOK*

This illustrated study guide is designed to reinforce the foundational truths and panoramic view of the Bible unfolded in the *KING OF GLORY* picture book and movie. To encourage and equip you to get the most out of this companion tool, let's first consider the **WHAT**, **WHEN**, **WHY**, **WHERE**, **WHO**, and **HOW** of the book and movie.

1. WHAT?

King of glory is one of God's hundreds of names, but it is also the title of the *KING OF GLORY* picture book and movie. The book has 70 Scenes, each with a one-page story and a full-page painting. These 70 stories fit together to tell ONE STORY. The movie (a word-for-word presentation of the book) groups the 70 Scenes into 15 Episodes. And what is THE STORY? The following description, taken from the DVD case, tells us:

KING of GLORY takes you on an intense ride through the Scriptures of the prophets as it chronologically and accurately unfolds their story and message in a way that makes sense. This 15-episode visualization of the world's best seller (the Bible) is about the Creator-Owner of the universe and His plan to rescue His rebel subjects from the kingdom of darkness and qualify them to live with Him forever in His kingdom of light. With its thought-provoking narrative and inspired mix of motion-graphics, still-animation, and live video, this film is for a worldwide audience of all ages.

2013-2014. The garage studio where the KING of GLORY video production took place.

2. WHEN?

It was in November 2009, while teaching the Scriptures in the Middle East, that God put into my heart the idea to produce an illustrated story book about the message of the prophets for people of all ages and worldviews. Working remotely for more than a year with an artist in Argentina, the *KING OF GLORY* picture book was published in September 2011. That same month, God planted in my mind the idea to turn the book into a movie. After working with a small creative team for nearly 4 years, the English *KING OF GLORY* movie was released in June 2015. Now, three years later (2018), the movie is in about 30 languages, with dozens more in planning or production.

3. WHY?

Amid the world's countless books and movies, what makes *KING OF GLORY* unique? **Why is it loved by a worldwide audience?** Here are some of their reasons:

1. "**I experienced the story** with all my emotions like I was actually there!"
2. "Great **culturally generic art**: no blue-eyed Moses or Jesus!"
3. "It draws out in a beautiful way **the magnificent story** that threads through the whole of Scripture."
4. "It pulls out **deep insights** that are fresh to a long-time student of Scripture and puts them in **simple terms** that even a novice can comprehend."
5. It presents a **panoramic view** of God's story in chronological order, showing how the many stories fit together to make one cohesive story.
6. It points out **foundational truths** about God, man, sin, and salvation, helping people connect the dots of Scripture and see the big picture of God's plan of redemption.
7. It includes **five Old Testament sacrifice stories** that prepare minds and hearts to understand why the Messiah had to die on the cross for our sins.
8. "It contains a beautiful 'distilling' of **the essential issues of the life of Christ**."
9. It is in **many languages**, with **free downloads**. www.king-of-glory.com
10. It captivates a **global audience** of **all ages**.
11. It is **ready to use**, with little or no preparation.
12. It gives people of all backgrounds a chance to meet and **fall in love with the King of glory Himself**.

"Love, love, love this!!!!"
— AMAZON CUSTOMER REVIEW, 2018

Another WHY question some ask is: **Why is the movie so long?**
Here are two answers:

1. Considering that the Bible takes about 70 hours to read aloud and that *KING OF GLORY* sums up its story and message in 3 hours and 42 minutes, *the movie is quite short!* And remember, it is divided into 15 episodes.
2. It takes time to tell God's story and message. While many people know bits and pieces of Scripture, most remain confused because they have never seen how the many parts of God's complex story fit together.

Now think about this: If you read a storybook to a child, where do you begin? In the middle? Near the end? No, you start at the beginning. Only then will the child understand the story. Likewise, to understand the Holy Scriptures, we must start at the beginning and follow the story to its logical and satisfying conclusion.

To illustrate the importance of this, imagine that I want to make God's story and message known to a group of people who don't know it. What if I were to tell them a later part of the story such as when the prophet John pointed to the Messiah and said, *"Look, the Lamb of God who takes away the sin of the world!"* (John 1:29). Would they understand the meaning of the prophet's announcement? Probably not! Why? Because I did not start at the beginning of God's book, which tells how the first man rebelled against his Maker, bringing upon humanity the law of sin and death, and how God in His justice and mercy revealed the law of the sacrifice, providing a temporary way for people's sin and shame to be covered until "the Lamb of God" came to earth with God's permanent solution for the problem of sin.

True, I just explained the backstory to John's Lamb-of-God announcement. But do you think people who know little or nothing about the Bible will understand such a brief, complex explanation? Probably not! They need to be told the story from the beginning. That is what the *KING OF GLORY* movie and picture book do.

4. WHERE?

In what settings are the *KING OF GLORY* chronological gospel-tools being used around the world? In homes, after-school programs, small group studies, Sunday school classes of all ages, kids clubs, youth camps, retirement centers, orphanages, refugee camps, immigrant support teams, waiting rooms, reading programs, ESL classes, social media, open air film showings, theaters, radio, and television broadcasts, websites, personal study…

Left: Girl at youth camp in Ecuador
Right: Boy at home in Kyrgyzstan

5. WHO?

Who are the *KING OF GLORY* movie and picture book for? Here is what my daughter Corrie, the mother of two of my six grandchildren, has to say:

*The teaching method in KING OF GLORY shows the big picture of the Bible in a way **kids** can really grasp.*

*For **adults**, it provides a framework for the entire Bible, so that when you read the Scriptures you understand how each part fits into the whole. **I love** the mystery element that makes you wonder how it will all pull together. I also like how it takes you into heaven at the end. **You see** that Jesus' victory was not only a big deal on earth, but also in heaven.*

*Although some scenes are intense, because the movie is not fully animated, it's **appropriate for younger kids**. They may get scared at some points, but it's a good kind of scared. The style of the artwork enhances the storytelling method.*

*The way it avoids showing the faces of Jesus and the prophets and incorporates darker skin tones makes it **applicable to any culture**. It's realistic, but artificial enough to keep you aware that it is an artist's rendition. It leaves room for the imagination. It is respectful to the Word of God, not cartoony. It has an artwork style that will age well.* — INTERVIEW WITH CORRIE MUTILVA, 2016

Watching *KING OF GLORY* in the Zarma language of Niger, West Africa.

6. HOW DOES THIS STUDY GUIDE WORK?

The *KING OF GLORY Illustrated Study Guide* is intended to reinforce the truths embedded in the 15-episode movie and/or the 70-scene picture book. An *Answer Key* and *Coloring Book* are also available at **www.king-of-glory.com** As you use these tools, it is helpful to keep in mind that *KING OF GLORY* tells the story and message of the Bible in a way that respects its **foundation** and **framework**.

THE FOUNDATION

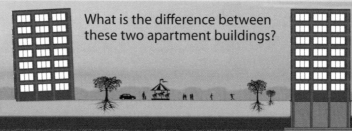

What is the difference between these two apartment buildings?

ABOVE GROUND VIEW
UNDER GROUND VIEW

From the outside, the above building may look good (or does it?), but it has no foundation. The foolish builders constructed it on top of the sand!

This building is anchored in bedrock. It was constructed by wise builders, *"who dug down deep and laid the foundation on rock"* (Luke 6:48).

In the Holy Scriptures, the King of the universe has provided a deep foundation for our faith. A crucial part of that deeply rooted foundation is *Genesis*, the first book of the Bible. *Genesis* tells us what actually happened in the beginning. Its first chapters are especially important, which is why the first 24 of 70 scenes in *KING OF GLORY* are based primarily on the first 4 chapters of *Genesis*. But *Genesis* is just a part of the Old Testament foundation God has laid to help us understand who He is and what He has done for us.

It is for good reason that our Creator-Redeemer revealed to His prophets the Old Testament Scriptures (*His Plan Foretold*) before He unveiled the New Testament Scriptures (*His Plan Fulfilled*). The *KING OF GLORY* movie and book build on the solid foundation of the Old Testament, which helps us understand God's plan to rescue sinners from the law of sin and death and give all who trust in Him a close relationship with Himself for time and eternity.

THE FRAMEWORK

The teaching method used in *KING OF GLORY* is somewhat like hanging laundry on a clothesline. The *clothesline* represents **the one big story** God wants us to understand. The *clothes in the basket* represents **the many stories** in the Bible. In our 15-episode journey from the beginning to the end of God's book, only some stories will be taken from "the basket" and hung on "the line." We will leave huge gaps, but enough will be put on the chronological line to reveal the framework of God's plan. Later, when you hear or read the rest of God's book, you will be able to understand where each part fits into the whole.

HOW TO USE THIS TOOL

Here are a few suggestions for using this study guide with different groups:

1. Oral Learners

Only the group leaders need the study guide as they take the participants through it orally. Be creative. Handle the study guide's questions in an interactive way. Perhaps you will have your group turn a story and its main point into a skit. To help the group remember what they have heard, the leader should be prepared to revisit scenes from the movie or picture book. The *KING OF GLORY Coloring Book* can also be a helpful addition in an oral learning environment.

2. Print Learners

Each person should have a copy of the study guide. The leader takes students through the discussion questions and/or exercises, and they write in their answers. This can also be used as a correspondence/home study course, where individuals watch each movie episode and fill in the answers on their own.

3. Time-Limited Groups

Some groups may only use the first two pages of each episode (*INTRODUCE, WATCH, DISCUSS, REFLECT*), skipping the *REINFORCE* section's exercises. This works well with adults, or when time is limited. Similarly, to keep a class from going too long, **the *REINFORCE* exercises could be used, and the *DISCUSS* questions skipped**.

4. English Learners (ESL)

LISTENING: Students watch the episode (with or without the English subtitles). COMPREHENSION & WRITING: Work through the questions and exercises. READING, PRONUNCIATION & VOCABULARY: Have students read some of the corresponding scenes in the *KING OF GLORY* picture book. Explain difficult words (like "mind-boggling" and "extravagant" used in Scene 1). The strength of these ESL tools is that they help students become fluent both in English *and* in God's plan for them for time and eternity!

GETTING MORE FROM THE JOURNEY

A. Begin at the beginning

The message from the one true God is embedded in His story. Treat it like a story. Don't skip around. Each new episode builds on information learned in previous episodes.

B. Stay on track

As you travel through *KING OF GLORY*, questions may arise which are not instantly answered. Make a note of such questions, but do not allow them to deter your group from moving forward and seeing THE BIG PICTURE. When you come to the end of the story, you can then search the Scriptures together to find God's answers to questions not answered in *KING OF GLORY*.[1] At the top of each scene is a book icon (📖) followed by the primary chapter(s) in the Bible on which the scene is based. Also, in the back of this book you will find a chart called "Related Scriptures" for further personal study.

C. Trust the Spirit of God to open minds and hearts

The ultimate purpose of the *KING OF GLORY* movie, picture book, study guide, and coloring book is to help people of all ages understand the foundational truths revealed in the Bible—about God, man (humanity), sin, and salvation.

My prayer to God is that the *KING OF GLORY* movie and/or book, along with this study guide, will inform and inspire you, your family, community, and nation to connect the dots in the Scriptures of the prophets, see God's plan, and grasp who you are and who you can be in His eyes, a*nd who the King of glory is and what He has done for you—"the righteous for the unrighteous, to bring you to God"* (1 Peter 3:18).

In Episode 12 (Scene 53 in the book), you will experience the story pictured below, a parable Jesus the Messiah told His disciples one day when they were on a mountain. Later, when a crowd had gathered at the foot of the mountain, He told it again.

"So why do you keep calling me 'Lord, Lord!' when you don't do what I say? I will show you what it's like when someone comes to me, listens to my teaching, and then follows it.

"It is like a person building a house who digs deep and lays the foundation on solid rock. When the floodwaters rise and break against that house, it stands firm because it is well built.

"But anyone who hears and doesn't obey is like a person who builds a house right on the ground, without a foundation. When the floods sweep down against that house, it will collapse into a heap of ruins" (Luke 6:46-49).

On what foundation are we building our lives?
Who is *your* foundation?

Prologue

"Who else has held the oceans
in his hand? Who has measured
off the heavens with his fingers?
Who else knows the weight
of the earth or has weighed
the mountains and hills on a scale?
To whom will you compare me?
Who is my equal?"
asks the Holy One.

Look up into the heavens.
Who created all the stars?
He brings them out like an army,
one after another, calling each
by its name.

—PROPHET ISAIAH (40:12, 25-26 NLT)

This mind-boggling NASA infrared composite image shows hundreds of thousands of stars in
the swirling center of our spiral Milky Way galaxy. What you see in this photo is about
800 light years across, just a small part of our galaxy, which is about 100,000 light years across.
When compared to the known universe, our Milky Way galaxy is tiny.
And when compared to the King who created and sustains it all, how big is the entire universe?
For the King's own answer, read the scroll above.

EPISODE 1
PROLOGUE

KING OF GLORY • SCENES 1–3

INTRODUCE

Would you like to travel through the ancient Scriptures of the prophets? Would you like to see how their many stories fit together to make *one* story (a story no human could have dreamed up)? Would you like to meet the awesome King who inspired them to write those stories? Would you like to know His plan *for you*?

As the eternal King's story stretches out before us, we will see our own story too. In this journey, we will hear His answers to life's big questions, such as:

"Where did I come from?"

"Why am I here?"

"Where will I end up?"

Only the One who lives above time can reveal the right answers. And where do we find those answers?

In the King's book.

This is the story and message from the One who has no beginning. It is about His extravagant plan to rescue His rebellious subjects from the kingdom of darkness and invite them to live with Him in His kingdom of light.

Do you know *His* story?
Do you know *yours*?

Watch (⏱10:40)

Episode 1 (in the *KING OF GLORY* movie) covers **Scenes 1-3** (in the *KING OF GLORY* book)

Discuss

1. What surprised you in this episode?

2. Based on what you just saw and heard, what impresses you most about the King of the universe?

3. How is the Bible different from all other books?

4. Which do you think is most reliable: the theories of people, or the Scriptures revealed to the prophets? Explain.

5. Do you believe that the first words of Scripture are absolutely true? Explain.

6. Would you like to personally get to know the One who made and maintains the universe? Explain.

Reflect (Meditate on, talk about this verse, and/or memorize it.)

Man does not live on bread alone but on every word that comes from the mouth of the LORD.
—Prophet Moses (Deuteronomy 8:3)

Reinforce

Starting on the next page, review what you heard in Episode 1 by doing the activities.

1 THE KING AND HIS KINGDOM

A **Fill in the blanks with the words from the box below. Use each word only once and cross it out after it is used.**

1. The __King of glory__ existed before the world began.

2. There was only _____ King and _____ kingdom, and it was perfect.

3. Rebellion arose in the kingdom, first in _____ , then on _____ .

> earth · ~~King of glory~~ · heaven · one · one

B **Based on what the Scripture teaches, answer these questions:**

1. Did the rebellion in His Kingdom surprise the King of the universe? How do you know this?

   _____

   _____

   _____

2. How long would the King take to fulfill His great, extravagant, mysterious rescue plan?

   _____

   _____

> For your kingdom is an everlasting kingdom.
> You rule throughout all generations.
> —PROPHET DAVID (PSALM 145:13 NLT)

2 THE KING AND HIS PROPHETS

To know the King and His plan, you must know His book.

A Connect the words and pictures with their definitions by drawing a line.

1. prophets / apostles

2. scrolls

3. the Holy Scriptures

a. an old kind of book; ancient copies of God's written word

b. the writings of the prophets and apostles; where we learn God's story and message

c. people God chose to write down His story and message

B The Scriptures are divided into two major parts. What are they? Write your answers on the lines labeled "1." and "2." below.

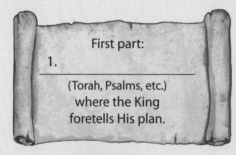

First part:

1. _____

(Torah, Psalms, etc.)
where the King
foretells His plan.

Second part:

2. _____

(Gospels, Acts, etc.)
where the King
fulfills His plan.

Between 1947 and 1956, more than 225 biblical manuscripts were discovered in 11 caves near the Dead Sea. These ancient scrolls, penned between 250 BC and AD 68, contain the same words as present-day Bibles, showing that the Old Testament Scriptures have been faithfully preserved.

C Answer the following questions:

1. How many years did God take to reveal His completed book?

   a. 20 years
   b. 500 years
   c. 7 centuries
   d. more than 15 centuries

2. How many people did He use to write His book?

   a. just one
   b. about 40
   c. four
   d. 124,000

3. What part of the world did the prophets come from?

   a. North America
   b. the Middle East
   c. Europe
   d. the Far East

4. Name one or more ways in which the Bible is different from all other books.

5. For whom did God give the Scriptures?

"Man does not live on bread alone but on every word that comes from the mouth of the LORD."
—PROPHET MOSES (TORAH/DEUTERONOMY 8:3)

3   THE KING AND HIS UNIVERSE

A   **Tell about one of these pictures. What does it teach you about the King and His Universe?**

_____

_____

_____

_____

B   **Circle the correct answer:**

1. According to the Scriptures (Genesis 1:1), where did the universe and everything in it come from?

    a. No one knows.

    b. By accident, when a hot speck of energy exploded and expanded, and later evolved life from mud to monkey to man.

    c. In the beginning (time), God created the heavens (space) and the earth (matter).

2. What does our beautiful, orderly universe teach us about our Creator?

    a. He is infinitely powerful and wise and worthy of our praise.

    b. There is no way to know that He even exists.

    c. Nothing.

C   **Based on what we have learned from the Scriptures, mark the following statements true or false.**

1. The King of glory created the universe.   (True) False

2. No one can know God in a personal way!   True   False

3. Your Creator wants you to know Him.   True   False

> For ever since the world was created, people have seen the earth and sky.
> Through everything God made, they can clearly see
> his invisible qualities—his eternal power and divine nature.
> So they have no excuse for not knowing God.
> ROMANS 1:20 NLT

Part 1

THE KING FORETELLS HIS PLAN

— OLD TESTAMENT —

Episode 2
The Creator & His Creation

KING of GLORY • Scenes 4–9

Introduce

Wthat does perfection look like? Do you know any*thing* that is perfect? Do you know any*one* who is perfect? We may aim for perfection, but we end up saying, *"Nobody's perfect!"*

Yet the Scriptures of the prophets tell of a King who is perfect. They also tell of a time in history when everything and everyone on earth was perfect.

Our journey begins where time began, as recorded on the first page of Holy Scripture, in the book of Genesis, chapter 1. Genesis means *origins* (*beginnings*). It is here that we first meet this perfect King, the One who has no beginning and no end. It is here that we begin to learn why He made humans.

If the Creator-Owner of the universe had not communicated His thoughts and desires to us, we could only guess where we came from, why we are here, and where we are going.

But the prophet Daniel wrote:

"He reveals deep and hidden things; he knows what lies in darkness, and light dwells with him" (Daniel 2:22).

Prepare to meet THE KING.

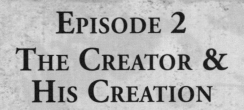

WATCH (🕐19:04)

Episode 2 covers **Scenes 4–9**

DISCUSS

1. What surprised you in this episode?

2. What did you learn about God in this episode?

3. What do you think is meant by this: "Even when He alone existed, He was never alone"?

4. What can we learn about God's character from the things He has made? (Six of God's characteristics are mentioned in Scene 5.)

5. Adam and Eve were created in the image of God. What does this mean?

6. Define sin and explain the connection between sin and death.

7. In the evenings, the LORD God would come into the garden to walk and talk with the man and his wife. What does this tell us about God?

REFLECT

In the beginning God created the heavens and the earth.
Then God said, "Let us make mankind in our image, in our likeness… ."
(Genesis 1:1, 26a)

REINFORCE

Review Episode 2 by doing the
activities on the following pages.

"He hangs the earth on nothing" (Prophet Job 26:7 NLT).
This Earthrise photo was taken on Christmas Eve 1968 by Apollo 8, the first manned mission to orbit the moon. That evening, the astronauts held a live broadcast from lunar orbit, ending the program with the crew reading from Genesis chapter 1.

4 THE FIRST DAY

📖 GENESIS 1

A   Circle the words that make this paragraph read correctly.

In the creation account we learn that God is the (*invisible*) / *visible* eternal
Spirit / *creature* who can be everywhere at once. He sees and knows
most things / *everything*. Even when He alone existed, He was never alone.
God is *light* / *darkness*, which means that He is pure and *perfect* / *imperfect*.
Another word for God's unique perfection is *holy* / *unholy*.

B   List the six characteristics of God which you circled above.

He is invisible	

C   Fill in the blanks using the words from the box below. Remember to use each word only once and cross it out after it is used.

1. The **name** of God which is most used in the Old Testament is
   the LORD or _____, which means *the One Who IS*,
   or simply *I AM*.

2. According to the Bible, _____ is the Source of light. First John 1:5
   says, "God is _____ ; in him there is no _____ at all."

3. God, His Holy Spirit, and His Word are _____ . His Holy Spirit and
   His Word were with God at _____ Genesis 1:1-3; John 1:1-3).
   His Holy Spirit was hovering over the waters as His Word _____
   light into the darkness.

> light · ~~name~~ · Yahweh · darkness
> one · God · creation · spoke

In the beginning was the Word,
and the Word was with God, and the Word was God.
He was with God in the beginning.
Through him all things were made;
without him nothing was made that has been made.
JOHN 1:1-3

D Answer the following questions.

1. How do the pictures above remind you of what God did on the first day of creation? Why do you think God chose to bring light into the world before He created the sun?

2. Name some ways in which God and light are similar. What does this teach us about God?

And God said, "Let there be light,"
and there was light.
GENESIS 1:3

5   A PERFECT WORLD

📖 GENESIS 1-2

In six days, the King created a beautiful, wonderful world. The six days of creation teach us some basic truths about our great Creator.

A   Look at the pictures and fill in the missing words with the words from the box below.

Day 1
God is **holy**.
He is perfect and pure, like *light*.

Day 2
God is _____.
He made and maintains the vast *atmosphere*.

Day 3
God is _____.
He created thousands of *plants* and *foods* for us to enjoy.

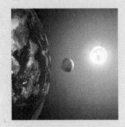

Day 4
God is _____.
The *sun, moon,* and *stars* always stay in their orbits.

Day 5
God is _____.
He created *fish* to swim in the sea and *birds* to fly in the sky.

Day 6
God is _____.
He created *humans* so that He could show them His love.

life · good · ~~holy~~ · love · faithful · all-powerful

God saw all that he had made, and it was very good. GENESIS 1:31

6 THE FIRST MAN

On the sixth day of Creation, the King made animals and people. Animals and people have some things in common, but they are also very different.

A Fill in the blanks to complete Genesis 1:26.

"God said, 'Let us make man in our _____, in our _____, and let them rule … over all the earth, and over all the creatures… .'"

B Answer the following questions.

1. What does it mean that humans were "made in the image of God"?

2. Name some ways God made humans different from animals.

3. What did God give to the first man and woman that made them distinctly different from the animals?

4. Did God plan for people to be His slaves or His friends? Explain.

5. God is not only the Creator of people; He is also their Owner. Explain.

7 A PERFECT HOME

📖 GENESIS 2

God made Adam to be the *head* of the human race and God's plan was for Adam and his family to *reign with Him forever*. This was a big task, but God started by giving Adam smaller tasks.

A **Connect the words with the definitions that best match them by drawing a line from left to right.**

1. Adam

2. Eve

3. Eden

4. Adam's first job

5. Adam's other job

a. the first home

b. the first woman

c. care for the garden

d. name the animals

e. the first man

B **Circle the words that best describe Adam and Eve's home. Circle more than one word.**

sad • (colorful) • delightful • perfect • dark • interesting • painful

C **Based on what we know about the garden of Eden and the LORD's interaction with Adam, what can we know about God?**

_____

_____

_____

_____

> The LORD God took the man
> and put him in the Garden
> of Eden to work it and take care of it.
> GENESIS 2:15

8 THE LAW OF SIN AND DEATH

📖 GENESIS 2

A Answer the following questions.

1. From the start, God and man were friends. Why did Adam's friendship with God need to be tested?

2. As a test, God gave Adam one rule to obey. What was that rule?

3. Was that rule difficult to obey? Why or why not?

4. What did God say would happen to Adam if he ate from the tree of the knowledge of good and evil? **(Circle the correct answer.)**
   a. Adam would need to do enough good deeds to outweigh his bad deeds.
   b. Adam would surely die.
   c. Adam would be obligated to recite daily prayers.

B Connect the words with the phrases that best match them. Both words (Sin & Death) will be used more than once.

a. disobedience to God's law

1. Sin

b. separation

c. an act of rebellion

2. Death

d. the penalty for breaking God's law

e. would end man's close friendship with God

The LORD God commanded the man, "You are free to eat from any tree in the garden; but you must not eat from the tree of the knowledge of good and evil, for when you eat of it you will surely die." GENESIS 2:16-17

9 THE FIRST WOMAN

📖 GENESIS 2

"God saw all that he had made, and it was very good" (Genesis 1:31).
At this point in history, the world was still a perfect place.

A **Mark the following statements true or false. Remember, if a statement is even *partly* wrong, circle the word "false."**

1. God arranged the first marriage. (True) False

2. God gave the man and his wife different roles, but He made them equal in value. True False

3. Both the man and the woman were made to know and love their Creator-Owner forever. True False

4. Adam and Eve felt afraid in God's presence. True False

5. Adam and Eve were both naked, but they felt no shame. True False

6. The one true God made people so He could have a close relationship with them. True False

7. God rested on the seventh day because He was tired. True False

B **Fill in the blanks using words from the box below.**

1. God said, "It is _____ that man should be alone. I will make a _____ suitable for him" (Genesis 2:18).

2. *Woman* means _____.

3. *Eve* means _____.

4. At the beginning of human history, there was a _____ couple, living in a _____ garden, enjoying friendship with their _____ Creator.

perfect • out of man • perfect • helper • not good • perfect • mother of all

SOMETHING TO THINK ABOUT

Days, months, and years are all related to astronomy (the physical universe):

a day = the earth rotates once every 24 hours
a month = the moon orbits the earth about every 30 days
a year = the earth orbits the sun once every 365 days

But **the week** is not based on the earth, moon, or sun.

Question: Where did the 7-day week come from?
Answer: Genesis 2:1-3 (See also: Exodus 20:11)

"God saw all that he had made, and it was very good. And there was evening, and there was morning—the sixth day. ... By the seventh day God had finished the work he had been doing; so on the seventh day he rested from all his work."

GENESIS 1:31; 2:2

Note: The sketches in this study guide are from the original, preliminary sketches drawn by our artist Arminda San Martín for the KING of GLORY 70-scene book. For more about this, see the "Behind the Scenes" introduction in the picture book.

EPISODE 3
EVIL'S ENTRANCE

KING OF GLORY • SCENES 10–15

INTRODUCE

God the LORD is great! He exists by His own power. You and I need air, water, food, sleep, and shelter to live, but our Creator needs nothing. He is the LORD. As we learned in the previous episode, His name means *I AM* or *HE IS*. Only a personal being can say, "I am." The eternal King of the universe wants us to know that He created people to enjoy a close relationship with Him forever. Awesome! But only holy people can live in His holy presence.

If the LORD God is perfect and holy, and if He made us to be like Him and with Him forever, then why are we not perfect and holy? Why can He seem so far away? Why do bad things happen in our world? Why do people sometimes hurt us? Why do we hurt others? Why do we have unholy thoughts? Why do we make bad choices? Why do we sin?

Where did sin come from? How did evil enter the King's perfect universe?

To learn God's answers, we will first explore what He has revealed in His book about angels and demons.

Prepare to visit a place of light and glory. Prepare to peer into a place of darkness and doom.

Get ready to discover the origin of sin.

WATCH (🕐15:10)

Episode 3 covers **Scenes 10-15**

DISCUSS

1. Did anything in the Bible's description of heaven surprise you?

2. What did you learn about angels in this episode?

3. In your own words, tell the biblical story of Lucifer's rebellion.

4. To help us understand what the devil is like, what do the Scriptures compare him to?

5. When the serpent spoke to Eve, how should she have responded?

6. When did Adam and his wife begin to feel shame? Did their self-made fig-leaf coverings make them feel comfortable in God's presence?

7. Using a branch, explain how Adam and his wife had become like a branch broken off a living tree.

8. What do we learn about God from the fact that He gave humans the freedom to choose between obeying Him and disobeying Him?

REFLECT

The LORD God commanded the man, "You are free to eat from any tree in the garden; but you must not eat from the tree of the knowledge of good and evil, for when you eat of it you will surely die." (Genesis 2:16-17)

"You will not surely die," the serpent said to the woman. (Genesis 3:4)

REINFORCE

Review Episode 3 by doing the activities on the following pages.

10 THE KINGDOM OF LIGHT

📖 REVELATION 4-5

What did you learn about Heaven in this episode?

A   Mark the following statements true or false.

1.   Heaven is also called Paradise.   (True) False

2.   Heaven is the King's home and reflects His glory.   True   False

3.   The King is all alone in Heaven.   True   False

4.   The best attraction in Heaven is the King Himself.   True   False

B   How much do you know about angels? Fill in the blanks using the words from the box below.

Angel means _____*messenger*_____ or *servant*. Before He made _____, the King of heaven made angels. They watched Him create the world. Angels are _____. Like their Creator, angels are _____ to man, except when sent on missions where they need to be seen. God gave His angels the capacity to _____ Him forever, but they were not God's _____. As with humans, God did not force them to _____ to Him. He wanted happy, willing servants.

> slaves · spirit beings · obey and serve
> · invisible · humans · ~~messenger~~ · submit

They encircled the throne … they never stop saying:
"Holy, holy, holy is the Lord God Almighty,
who was, and is, and is to come."
REVELATION 5:11, 4:8

11 THE KINGDOM OF DARKNESS

📖 ISAIAH 14; EZEKIEL 28

A Connect the beginning of each sentence with the correct ending.

1. Lucifer means …   a. … hell.
2. Satan means …   b. … deceiver.
3. Devil means …   c. … accuser.
4. A demon is an …   d. … evil angel.
5. The Lake of Fire is also called …   e. … Shining One.

B Mark the following statements true or false.

1. When God made him, Lucifer was one of God's   True   False
   chief angels: full of wisdom and perfect in beauty.

2. Lucifer became proud of himself   True   False
   and wanted to be king!

3. Lucifer convinced all the angels   True   False
   to join his rebellion against God.

4. God immediately threw Satan and   True   False
   all the rebellious angels into hell.

5. God threw Satan and his demons out of heaven   True   False
   and down to Earth's atmosphere.

Satan disguises himself
as an angel of light.
2 CORINTHIANS 11:14 NLT

12 THE SERPENT

📖 GENESIS 3

A Answer the following questions.

1. Who came each evening into the garden for a personal visit with Adam and Eve? Do you think they enjoyed His visits? Why or why not?

_____

_____

_____

2. Who came to the garden to visit Eve and spoke to her through a serpent?

_____

3. Which visitor told the truth and wanted what was best for Adam and Eve?

_____

4. Which one told lies and wanted to destroy them?

_____

B Why did Satan come to the garden?
Mark the following statements about Satan true or false.

1. Satan wanted Adam to choose to break God's law. (True) False

2. Satan wanted Eve to trust God's word. True False

3. Satan wanted Eve to think that God was keeping something good from her and her husband. True False

4. Satan told Eve that if she disobeyed God she would die. True False

13 THE CHOICE

📖 GENESIS 3

A Fill in the blanks with words from the box below.

1. "You must not eat from the tree of the knowledge of _good_
    and _____, for when you eat of it you will surely
    _____." — *The LORD* (Genesis 2:16-17)

2. "You will _____ surely die." —*Satan* (Genesis 3:4)

3. Scripture explains why Eve was tempted to take and eat the forbidden
    fruit. It says that she saw that the fruit was good for _____,
    pleasing to the _____ and desirable for gaining _____.

> eye • wisdom • ~~good~~ • evil • not • die • food

B Mark the following statements about the LORD true or false.

1. The LORD had given Adam and Eve freedom to choose   True   False
    between doing His will or their own will.

2. The LORD wanted Adam and Eve to trust Him, even   True   False
    when they didn't understand the reasons for His rule.

3. When Adam chose to disobey, only the LORD knew   True   False
    the terrible, far-reaching consequences of his sin.

> "Did God really say, 'You must not eat
> from any tree in the garden'?"
> GENESIS 3:1

> "You will *not* surely die."
> GENESIS 3:4

> Then the eyes of both of them were opened, and they realized
> they were naked; so they sewed fig leaves together and
> made coverings for themselves. GENESIS 3:7

14 SIN AND SHAME

📖 GENESIS 3

After Adam and Eve sinned, many things changed.

A **Connect the words on the left with the words that mean the opposite, on the right.**

1.	honor	a.	unclean
2.	holy	b.	shame
3.	naked	c.	guilty
4.	God-conscious	d.	enemy
5.	innocent	e.	self-conscious
6.	clean	f.	sinful
7.	friend	g.	covered
8.	confident/happy	h.	afraid

B **Use the words from above to tell about the before and after of Adam and Eve's story.**

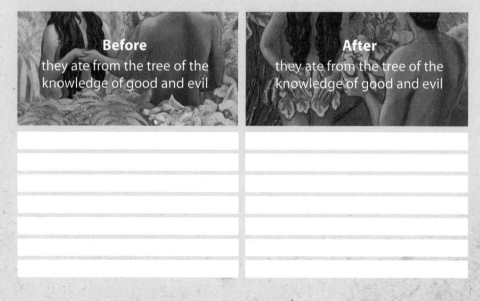

Before
they ate from the tree of the knowledge of good and evil

After
they ate from the tree of the knowledge of good and evil

15 SPIRITUALLY DEAD

📖 GENESIS 3

A Who said what? Fill in the name of the person who is speaking in this conversation. There are three different speakers.

1. _____ : "Where are you?"

2. _____ : "I heard You in the garden, and I was afraid because I was naked; so I hid."

3. _____ : "Who told you that you were naked? Have you eaten from the tree from which I commanded you not to eat?"

4. _____ : "The woman you put here with me—she gave me some fruit from the tree, and I ate it."

5. _____ : "What is this you have done?"

6. _____ : "The serpent deceived me, and I ate."

(Genesis 3:9-13)

B Answer the following questions.

1. Before they disobeyed God, Adam and Eve rejoiced to see their Creator-Friend each time He came to visit them. How did this change after they sinned? What did they try to do when He came to visit?

_____

_____

_____

2. Adam and Eve no longer mirrored the holy image of God. Instead of reflecting their Creator's holiness and love, what did they now reflect?

_____

_____

C Sin brought death and destruction. Some of the changes were obvious right away and some were not. Fill in the blanks using the words from the box below.

The first couple had become like a _____ broken off a living tree. Their _____ had broken off their _____ with the King of the universe. _____ they were dead. Their sin had separated them from the Source of _____. _____, they were still _____, but the process of growing old had begun. Death's power had invaded their bodies.

> relationship • alive • branch • sin • spiritually • physically • eternal life

But your iniquities have
separated you from your God;
your sins have hidden
his face from you ....

ISAIAH 59:2

Episode 4
Sin's Curse & God's Promise
KING of GLORY • Scenes 16–19

Introduce

To fly, which wing does a bird need? The left or the right? We all know that a bird needs both wings to fly! Anyone who thinks that a bird can fly with just one wing is ignoring *the design of birds* (aerodynamics) and *the law of gravity*.

Similarly, anyone who thinks that the King of the universe can show *mercy* to sinners without administering *justice* is ignoring *the holy nature of God* and *the law of sin and death*.

Because *God is holy,* He must judge sin.

But because *God is love,* He wants to show mercy to sinners.

How can He do both?

As human beings, if we sin against someone, and we ask them to forgive us, they may respond, "No problem. It's OK. I forgive you." But our Creator-Judge never says, "No problem. I love you, so I won't judge your sin." But neither does He say, "Since you have sinned, I don't love you." The righteous Judge of all the earth loves people, but He must uphold His laws. He must judge all sin. So how can He show *mercy* to sinners without ignoring His holy nature that demands *justice*?

As we continue the story of our disobedient first parents, we will begin to learn about the King's plan to punish their sin without punishing them. We will see that on the same sad, dark day that Adam and Eve sinned against their Creator-Owner, He gave them a glimmer of hope.

WATCH (🕐11:57)

Episode 4 covers **Scenes 16-19**

DISCUSS

1. What surprised you in this episode?

2. What did you learn about God in this episode?

3. Were thorns, sadness, sickness, and death a part of God's original creation? Explain.

4. Explain the effect of sin on a human's relationship with God.

5. Name and explain the three terrible separations caused by sin.

6. What is the law of sin and death?

7. On the day Adam and Eve sinned, what great promise did God make?

8. On that same day, what did God do to show Adam and Eve His justice, mercy, and grace?

REFLECT

"And I will cause hostility between you and the woman,
and between your offspring and her offspring.
He will strike your head, and you will strike his heel."
(Genesis 3:15 NLT)

And the LORD God made clothing from
animal skins for Adam and his wife.
(Genesis 3:21 NLT)

REINFORCE

Reinforce Episode 4 by doing the activities on the following pages.

16 THE CURSE

GENESIS 3

A Answer the following questions.

1. Based on what we just learned (from Genesis 3), what bad and sad things would Adam and Eve experience on earth because of their sin?

2. Name some ways that sin's curse affects your life.

B Sin produces three terrible separations (deaths). What are they?

1.

Spiritual Death

Man's spirit separated from God.

2.

Man's spirit and soul separated from his body— and from his loved ones.

3.

Man's spirit, soul, and body *forever separated from God*—in the Lake of Fire

"Dust you are and to dust you will return."
GENESIS 3:19

17 THE PROMISE

📖 GENESIS 3

A   Tell about what you see in this picture.

4

B   Answer the following questions.

1.   What curse did God put on the serpent?
     What curse did God put on Satan?

2.   When God cursed Satan, He also began to make known His secret plan
     to rescue people from Satan, sin, and death. What did God promise?

"I will put enmity between you and the woman,
and between your offspring and hers; he will crush your head,
and you will strike his heel." GENESIS 3:15

18 THE FIRST SACRIFICE

📖 GENESIS 3

A Answer the following questions.

1. Adam and Eve made coverings of fig leaves for themselves after they disobeyed God. Why did their leaf coverings not make them feel comfortable in the presence of their Creator-Judge?

2. Who made the first animal sacrifice? Why did Adam and Eve need a substitute to die in their place?

B Fill in the blanks on the right with the words from box below that go with the matching description and picture.

1. The law of sin and death must be upheld. Sin must be punished with death.

2. God provided animals to die in Adam and Eve's place. God punished their sin without punishing them.

3. God showed Adam and Eve undeserved kindness by dressing them in the skins of the sacrificed animals.

Grace • Justice • Mercy

"I am overwhelmed with joy in the LORD my God!
For he has dressed me with the clothing of salvation
and draped me in a robe of righteousness." Isaiah 61:10 NLT

19 BANISHED

📖 GENESIS 3

A   Mark the following statements about God true or false.

1.   God had a plan to rescue humans if they would trust Him.   (True)   False

2.   God put the man and his wife out of the earthly paradise.   True   False

3.   God does not need to punish sin.   True   False

4.   God must enforce the laws that He has decreed.   True   False

5.   God cannot lie or go back on His word.   True   False

B   Answer the following questions.

1.   The LORD God guarded the way to the tree of life. Why did God not want Adam and Eve to eat from the tree of life after they sinned?

_____

_____

_____

2.   What are some other words that mean the same thing as "holy"?

_____

_____

> "I will not break my covenant;
> I will not take back a single word. ...
> In my holiness I cannot lie." PSALM 89:34-35 NLT

EPISODE 5
THE WAY OF THE SACRIFICE
KING OF GLORY • SCENES 20–24

INTRODUCE

I f a branch is broken from a tree, is it dead or alive? It may look alive for a while, but the truth will soon be obvious. It is dead! As we learned in the last three episodes, *death* means *separation*—separation from the Source of life.

Look again at the branch that has been separated from its tree. If the dying leaves on the broken branch could talk, they might say, "It's not our fault that the branch got broken off the tree!" But we know that the entire branch is doomed.

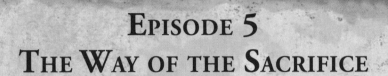

In a similar way, like it or not, each one of us was born into Adam's broken family, separated from our holy Creator.

The prophet David wrote, *"I was born a sinner—yes, from the moment my mother conceived me"* (Psalm 51:5 NLT).

Today, some people will tell you that babies are born pure, without a sin-bent nature. But the Scriptures teach us that when Adam broke God's law, the entire human family was affected by Adam's sin.

But as we learned in the last episode, God had a plan to cancel out *the law of sin and death* and make a way to save Adam's descendants from the curse of sin. This next story about the world's first kids will help us better understand that plan.

WATCH (🕐14:58)

Episode 5 covers **Scenes 20–24**

DISCUSS

1. Using a broken branch, explain how Cain and Abel were affected by their parents' sin.

2. What did you learn about God from how He dealt with Cain and Abel?

3. Tell about the kind of offering God required to cover sin and accept worship.

4. Explain how *the law of the sin offering* set Abel free from *the law of sin and death*.

5. Why was God not satisfied with Cain's offering?

6. Explain what *atonement* means.

7. Explain what *repentance* means.

8. In what ways were Cain and Abel alike, and in what ways were they different? Would you rather be like Cain or like Abel? Explain.

REFLECT

When Adam sinned, sin entered the world. Adam's sin brought death, so death spread to everyone, for everyone sinned. (Romans 5:12 NLT)

Without the shedding of blood there is no forgiveness. (Hebrews 9:22)

REINFORCE

Review Episode 5 by doing the activities on the following pages.

20 THE FIRST CHILDREN

📖 GENESIS 4

A Tell about what life was like outside the garden of Eden.

B Mark the following statements true or false.

1. There was no happiness or joy outside the garden.   True   (False)

2. Eve named their first sons Cain and Abel.   True   False

3. Cain and Abel had sinful natures like their parents.   True   False

C Fill in the blanks using the words from the box below.

1. Eve said, "With the help of the LORD I have brought forth a
   _____" (Genesis 4:1).

2. "Adam … had sons and daughters … in his own likeness,
   in his own _____"(Genesis 5:4,3).

3. "When Adam _____, sin entered the world. Adam's
   sin brought death, so _____ spread to everyone, for
   everyone _____" (Romans 5:12 NLT).

4. "I was born a _____—yes, from the moment my
   mother conceived _____" (Psalm 51:5 NLT).

> death · sinned · image · man · sinner · me · sinned

D How do these two pictures remind you that every member of Adam's family is a sinner?

21 SINNERS WORSHIP

📖 GENESIS 4

A Put a check mark under the name of the brother to which each phrase applies. Some phrases apply to both brothers, some to only one.

	Cain	Abel
1. Son of Adam and Eve	✔	✔
2. Kept flocks of sheep		
3. Worked the soil		
4. Wanted his Creator to accept him		
5. A sinner		
6. Brought a firstborn lamb as an offering to God		
7. Respected the law of sin and death		

B What kind of offerings does God require and accept? Mark the following statements true or false.

1. Both Cain and Abel had the same problem, which was sin.   (True) False

2. God told Cain and Abel that if they would fast and pray, then He would forgive them of their sins.   True   False

3. God said that without the shedding of blood there is no forgiveness of sins. Sin must be punished with death.   True   False

4. Sinners deserve to die, but God said He would accept the blood of certain animals, such as a lamb, to cover their sins.   True   False

5. The lamb offered could be sick or scratched or dirty.   True   False

6. The lamb would be killed as the sinner's substitute.   True   False

5

22 The Law of the Sin Offering

📖 GENESIS 4

"God always upholds justice but wants to show mercy. How could He punish sin without punishing the sinner?"— From Scene 22

A Answer the following questions.

1. What is an altar? What happens on an altar?

2. What does *atonement* mean?

B In Old Testament times, God told people that He would accept the shed blood of certain animals as a temporary payment for sins. Circle the kinds of animals whose blood God would accept.

(lambs) pigs · horses · goats · bulls · dogs · doves · camels

C Fill in the blanks with the words from the box below.

1. The life of a creature is in the _____, and I have given it to you to make _____ for yourselves on the altar; it is the blood that makes atonement for one's life (Leviticus 17:11).

2. He is to lay his hand on the head of the _____, and it will be accepted on his behalf to make _____ for him (Leviticus 1:4).

> atonement · blood · burnt offering · atonement

D Explain how Abel was set free from the law of sin and death.

23 ACCEPTED AND REJECTED

📖 GENESIS 4

A Look at the pictures below and explain why the LORD rejected one offering and not the other.

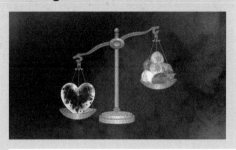 

5

B Put a check mark under the name of the brother to which each phrase applies. Each phrase applies to only one of the brothers.

	Cain	Abel
1. Offering was accepted by God		✔
2. Offering was rejected by God	✔	
3. Did not trust in the LORD's plan		
4. Trusted in the LORD's plan		
5. Forgiven and declared righteous		
6. Would know God as his Friend		
7. Would face God as his Judge		
8. In a right relationship with God		
9. Religious, but not in a right relationship with God		

24 THE FIRST MURDER

📖 GENESIS 4-5

A   Mark the following statements true or false.

1.   To repent means to punish yourself for your sins.   True   (False)

2.   To repent means to change your mind.   True   False

3.   To repent means to see your sin as God sees it.   True   False

4.   God wanted Cain to repent.   True   False

5.   Cain chose to repent and to follow God's way.   True   False

B   Explain what you see in this picture. How did Cain respond when the LORD refused his offering? What did Cain do when the LORD gave him a chance to repent? Where is Cain going?

The Lord is ... patient with you, not wanting anyone to perish,
but everyone to come to repentance. 2 PETER 3:9

"Without the shedding of blood
there is no forgiveness."
HEBREWS 9:22

5

EPISODE 6
MAN'S REBELLION & GOD'S FAITHFULNESS
KING OF GLORY • SCENES 25–27

INTRODUCE

Let's be honest. When it comes to spiritual truth, we are slow learners. But the King of the universe is a patient Teacher. That is why He includes hundreds of stories in His book to help us to see and understand this elementary truth: *"Without the shedding of blood there is no forgiveness"* (Hebrews 9:22).

From the day sin entered the world, the LORD God began to show sinners that only the blood of a suitable substitute could atone for (cover) sin. That is how He satisfied the law of sin and death and showed mercy to sinners.

The LORD rejected Adam and Eve's efforts to cover their sin, but put innocent animals to death in their place. The blood covered their sin and the animal skin clothing covered their shame.

In the last episode, we saw how Abel honored God and satisfied the strict demands of the law of sin and death by offering to God the blood of a healthy, perfect lamb. Meanwhile, Cain ignored God's way of forgiveness. And when the LORD gave him the chance to repent, he refused to submit to God's plan.

It is time to see what happened to the descendants of Cain and the ancient world in the days of the prophet Noah.

It is time to experience and learn from the most catastrophic global event in world history.

WATCH (🕐9:05)

Episode 6 covers **Scenes 25–27**

DISCUSS

1. Explain what the human condition was like ten generations after Adam.

2. How did God show both justice and mercy in the time of Noah?

3. What does the flood teach us about the patience and judgment of God?

4. Tell what happened at Babel. What can you learn from this event?

5. Think back to the stories we have heard about creation, Lucifer, Adam and Eve, Cain and Abel, the world in Noah's day, and the events at Babel. What have these stories revealed about God? About people?

REFLECT

In the six hundredth year of Noah's life, on the seventeenth day of the second month—on that day all the springs of the great deep burst forth, and the floodgates of the heavens were opened. (Genesis 7:11)

"Geological and fossil records affirm the biblical record. From the Sahara to the Himalayas, marine fossils can be unearthed in the world's great deserts and mountains." —From Episode 6, Scene 25

Ringwoodite [2]

Bryce Canyon, Utah, is one of thousands of distinct locations around the world that displays the effects of erosion caused by the waters of the global flood, which dissolved soil and rock, carried away the debris along with dead plants and animals, and laid down rock layers with trillions of fossils.

REINFORCE

Review Episode 6 by doing the activities on the following pages.

25 PATIENCE AND JUDGMENT

📖 GENESIS 6-7

A Each picture represents a historical event that is described below in numbers 1 to 6. Label each picture with the number from the matching description.

1. God saw that *"the wickedness of man was great on the earth, and ... the thoughts of his heart [were] only evil all the time"* (Genesis 6:5).

2. Noah found favor in the eyes of the LORD. He trusted God.

3. God told Noah that He would destroy all people with a flood. He told Noah to build a three-level ark. This ark would preserve Noah, his family, and a pair of each kind of animal, plus seven pairs of animals that were fit for sacrifice.

4. When the ark was finally ready, God brought to it a pair of each kind of animal, reptile, insect, and bird. Noah's family were the only people who accepted the refuge of the ark.

5. God shut the door of the ark. Everyone and everything inside was safe. Everyone outside the ark was doomed.

6. Fountains of water gushed up from deep down in the earth. Rain fell on the earth for forty days and forty nights. The flood was the worst natural disaster in history.

He did not spare the ancient world when he brought the flood on its ungodly people, but protected Noah ... and seven others .... 2 PETER 2:5

B   What does the flood event teach us about God and what He is like?

It was by faith that Noah built a large boat to save his family
from the flood. He obeyed God, who warned him about
things that had never happened before.
By his faith Noah condemned the rest of the world,
and he received the righteousness that comes by faith.
HEBREWS 11:7 NLT

6

26 A Fresh Start

📖 GENESIS 8-9

A Answer the following questions.

1. What happened to Noah and his family, and to the animals in the ark?

2. Approximately how long were Noah and his family in the ark?
   - a. 40 days
   - b. one year ⟵ (circled)
   - c. 400 days
   - d. three years

3. Where is Mount Ararat (where the ark landed)?
   - a. Morocco
   - b. China
   - c. Syria
   - d. Turkey

4. What was the first thing Noah did after his family and the animals came out of the ark?
   - a. built new homes
   - b. planted crops
   - c. sacrificed burnt offerings
   - d. sent out a dove

5. After the flood, what did God command Noah and his family to do?

6. After the flood, what was the covenant the LORD God made with the earth, and what was the symbol of the covenant?

He who promised
is faithful. HEBREWS 10:23

27 THE TOWER OF PRIDE

📖 GENESIS 11

A Answer the following questions.

1. Even when blessed with a fresh start, within a few generations most
    people had turned away from the LORD to go their own way.
    For example, God had commanded mankind to spread out and "fill the
    earth" (Genesis 1:28; 9:1). But what did man do instead, and why?

6

_____

_____

_____

_____

2. What did the builders of the tower have in common with Satan?
    What did they have in common with Cain?

_____

_____

_____

_____

3. How did God respond to the building project?
    What happened to the builders and their families?

_____

_____

_____

> God opposes the proud,
> but shows favor to the humble.
> JAMES 4:6

EPISODE 7
GOD'S PLAN ADVANCES

KING OF GLORY • SCENES 28–32

INTRODUCE

To this day, many people in many lands continue to offer animal sacrifices, but most don't know where the idea came from or what it meant. They have not yet understood that sacrifices of innocent animals were only pictures and symbols that pointed to a future, final Sacrifice which God Himself would provide, *"so that everyone who believes may have eternal life in him"* (John 3:15).

Some ask, does God still want us to sacrifice lambs for our sins? The answer is, "No." And why not? Because more than 2000 years ago, God sent His perfect "Lamb" into the world. Two episodes from now, we will begin to read about Him, but first we must see a few more pictures and hear a few more prophecies about this wonderful Savior of whom the prophets wrote in the Scriptures.

This episode is about the prophet Abraham. In the book of Genesis, the first book of the Torah of Moses, there are many chapters about Abraham. In this episode, we cannot read all those stories, but we will tell some of the most important ones.

It is time to hear the story of the prophet Abraham through whom the LORD planned to create a nation from which would come
> the prophets,
> > the Scriptures,
> > > and the Savior of the world.

> It is time to learn more about
> > the King and His rescue plan.

WATCH (🕐14:04)

Episode 7 covers **Scenes 28–32**

DISCUSS

1. What was the human condition ten generations after Noah?

2. What two promises did God make to Abram (Abraham)?

3. What impressed you about God's covenant with Abraham?

4. How would you feel if God asked you to leave your family, country, and religion to follow Him? How would you respond?

5. Tell about a time when Abraham and Sarah trusted God, and a time when they didn't.

6. Why did God declare Abraham righteous?

7. What can we learn from Abraham's sacrifice on Mount Moriah?

8. Why did Abraham's son not die on the altar?

9. Why did Abraham name the mountain "The LORD **Will Provide**"?

REFLECT

So Abraham called that place
The LORD Will Provide.
And to this day it is said,
"On the mountain of the LORD
it will be provided." (Genesis 22:14)

This rocky hill, called *The Place of the Skull*, located outside Jerusalem's northern wall, is a part of the Moriah mountain range where Abraham offered up the ram in the place of his son.

REINFORCE

Review Episode 7 by doing the activities on the following pages.

28 GOD CALLS ABRAHAM

📖 GENESIS 12

A Mark the following statements true or false.

1. About 10 generations passed between the time of   (True) False
   Noah and Abraham.

2. When God called Abraham, he and his wife had   True   False
   children but no grandchildren.

3. Abraham and his wife Sarah's parents and neighbors True   False
   were idolaters. Instead of trusting in the LORD,
   they trusted in their man-made religions.

4. To trust and obey God is always easy.   True   False

B One day the LORD spoke to Abraham. What did He say? Fill in the blanks with the words from the box below.

"Leave your country, your people and your _____ and
go to the _____ I will show you. "I will make you into a great
_____ and I will _____ you; I will make your
name great, and you will be a _____ . I will bless those who
bless you, and whoever curses you I will curse; and _____
on earth will be blessed through you" (Genesis 12:1-3).

> bless • all peoples • father's household • nation • blessing • land

C Answer the following questions.

1. If Abraham would leave his father's family and go to an unknown land,
   what did the LORD promise to do for him? What did the LORD promise to
   do for the rest of the world through Abraham and his family?

   _____

   _____

   _____

2. How did Abraham respond to God's instructions? (Hint: Hebrews 11:8.)

   _____

   _____

   _____

Abraham believed God,
and it was credited to him as righteousness,
and he was called God's friend.
JAMES 2:23

7

29 THE PROMISE KEEPER

📖 GENESIS 15-17, 21

A   Answer the following questions.

1. How did Abraham react to God's "impossible" promise to give him a son despite his old age, and make him the father of a great nation?

    a. Abraham doubted God.   b. Abraham believed God.

    c. Abraham questioned God.   d. Abraham dishonoured God.

2. Were Abraham and Sarah sinners?
    How could God declare them righteous?

3. How did Abraham and Sarah wrongly try to "help" God fulfill His promise to give Abraham a son?

4. What was the name of the son of Abraham and Hagar?

    a. Isaac   b. Ishmael

5. What was the name of the "son of the promise," Sarah's only son?

    a. Isaac   b. Ishmael

6. Why did Abraham and his family have the practice of sacrificing lambs on altars for their sins?

68

30 THE ULTIMATE TEST

📖 GENESIS 22

A Explain what you see in this picture of Abraham and his son.
Where are they going? Why?

_____

_____

_____

_____

_____

_____

_____

_____

_____

_____

_____

_____

_____

B Mark the following statements true or false.

1. God planned to use Abraham and his son to set before   True   False
    the world a picture of His plan to rescue sinners.

2. God tested Abraham's faith to the extreme.   True   False

3. God told Abraham to sacrifice a ram on the altar,   True   False
    and to take along his son to help.

C Isaac asked his father Abraham, "Where is the lamb for the burnt
offering?" What was Abraham's reply?

_____

_____

_____

31 THE CONDEMNED SON

📖 GENESIS 22

A Answer the following questions.

1. Abraham believed that God had promised to make Isaac the father of a new nation, and he knew that God cannot …

    a. love
    b. hate
    c. lie
    d. heal

2. Before he and his son climbed the mountain, Abraham told his servants, "We will worship and then we will come back to you." How could Abraham's son *come back* if he was to be killed and his body burned?

3.   When they reached the place God had told him about, what did Abraham build? What did he do to his son?

4. Abraham's son was bound on the altar. Like all of Adam's descendants, he was a sinner and condemned to die for his sins. What did God provide that day to save Abraham's son from the law of sin and death?

> Abraham looked up and there in a thicket
> he saw a ram caught by its horns.
> He went over and took the ram and sacrificed it
> as a burnt offering instead of his son.
> GENESIS 22:13

32 PICTURES AND PROPHECIES

📖 GENESIS 22

A Answer the following questions.

1. Why did Abraham name the mountain *The LORD Will Provide* instead of *The LORD Has Provided*? (Hint: John 8:56.)

2. How did the provision of a ram to die in the place of Abraham's son picture God's plan for the holy Savior He would send to earth?

7

So Abraham called that place *The LORD Will Provide*.
And to this day it is said, "On the mountain
of the LORD it will be provided."
GENESIS 22:14

EPISODE 8
THE LAW & THE PROPHETS
KING of GLORY • SCENES 33–36

INTRODUCE

Before we finish the first stage of our journey (which has given us a panoramic view of the Old Testament Scriptures), let's pause and think about this King we have been getting to know and about His way of bringing sinners back to Himself. He is holy and His way of forgiveness flows from His perfect nature. People contaminated by sin cannot dwell in His presence. Washing our hands and feet does not cleanse our hearts, nor does trying to do more good than bad.

 The Holy Scriptures declare,
"Without holiness no one will see the Lord…
For our God is a consuming fire" (Hebrews 12:14, 29).

We all know that for things to survive in a fire, they must have certain qualities. For example, gold and silver can survive a blazing fire, but wood and paper cannot.

 Likewise, Adam's sin-contaminated descendants cannot survive in God's presence unless they are first forgiven and declared righteous by God.

As we conclude the first part of the King's book, we need to hear a few more stories about our holy God who invites sinners such as you and me to dwell with Him, but only if His righteous requirements are met.

It is time to learn some great truths from the Law and the prophets, which God gave to His ancient people—to bless you and me!

WATCH (🕐 12:20)

Episode 8 covers **Scenes 33–36**

DISCUSS

1. What does *holy* mean? Who is holy, and who is not?

2. We can try hard to obey God's rules, but can we ever be good enough to qualify to live with God in heaven? Why or why not?

3. How many of the Ten Commandments can you name? In what way are those ten rules like a mirror?

4. In what way do the Ten Commandments show us that we need a Savior?

5. Why did the Israelites bring lambs to altars? What could the blood of an animal do for the sin of the people? What could it *not* do?

6. Name some facts that the prophets foretold about the coming Messiah-Savior-King.

7. In thinking over our journey through the Old Testament Scriptures (Episodes 1 to 8), tell about one story or lesson that touched you.

REFLECT

No one will be declared righteous in his sight by observing the law; rather, through the law we become conscious of sin. (Romans 3:20)

The virgin will conceive a child! She will give birth to a son and will call him Immanuel (which means 'God is with us'). (Isaiah 7:14 NLT)

REINFORCE

Review Episode 8 by doing the activities on the following pages.

The pyramids and Sphinx of Egypt had already existed for 1,000 years when God delivered His people from their slavery and brought them to Mount Sinai where He organized them into the nation through which would come the prophets, the Scriptures, and the Savior of the world.

33 A Faithful and Holy God

📖 EXODUS 19-20

A **What were the two big promises the LORD had made to Abraham?**

_____

_____

Abraham had Isaac, Isaac had Jacob, and Jacob had twelve sons whose families became the twelve tribes of Israel. Around 1500 BC, God called Moses, Abraham's descendant, to be His prophet.

B **Connect each event from Moses' life with the related picture.**

1. Moses wrote the first five books of the Bible (the Torah).

   a.

2. Moses led Abraham's descendants away from slavery in Egypt.

   b.

3. God Himself guided this new nation through the desert with a cloud.

   c.

4. God opened a path of escape for them in the Red Sea.

   d.

5. God gave them bread from heaven.

   e.

6. God gave them water from a rock, and brought them to Mount Sinai.

   f.

C **Fill in the blanks with the words from the box below.**

1. "You will be for me a _____ …
   and a _____ nation!" (Exodus 19:6).

2. "Mount Sinai was covered with _____ , because the LORD descended on it in _____ " (Exodus 19:18 NLT).

> fire • smoke • kingdom • holy

D **Which heart represents sinfulness, and which represents holiness? Which kind of heart did the people of Israel think they had?**

_____
_____
_____
_____
_____
_____

a.

b.

E **Mark the following statements true or false.**

1. To be holy means to be set apart for God, or distinct. True False

2. The people understood what it meant to be holy. True False

3. The people *thought* they could earn God's favor. True False

4. At Mount Sinai, God showed His anger against sin. True False

5. God gave ten rules to Adam, and one rule to this new nation. True False

8

📖 EXODUS 20

A **Write out the Ten Commandments (in brief) on the stone tablets.**
Check Exodus 20 or Episode 8 (Scene 34 of the *KING OF GLORY* book) for help.

Whoever keeps the whole law and yet stumbles at
just one point is guilty of breaking all of it. JAMES 2:10

B   Mark the following statements true or false.

1. God chose the people in this new nation because they were so good and holy.   True   False

2. God told Moses that they must obey all ten rules perfectly.   True   False

3. The people were able to obey all ten rules perfectly.   True   False

4. God sees the sin in our hearts.   True   False

5. Because God is holy, He cannot ignore sin.   True   False

6. Doing good deeds can cleanse our hearts.   True   False

7. The Ten Commandments can cleanse our hearts.   True   False

C   Answer the following questions.

1. How do you think the people felt after they heard the Ten Commandments?

2. How are God's rules or laws like a mirror?

3. If observing the law of God cannot cleanse from sin, what then is the purpose of the law?

4. Do you think you are good enough to live in God's perfect kingdom? Why or why not?

8

35 MORE PICTURES

📖 EXODUS 20, 24

The Ten Commandments gave the new nation both good and bad news.

A   Answer the following questions.

1.   What *bad news* did God's Law bring to the people?
     What *good news* did God's Law bring to the people?

2.   Explain how, in the time before the Savior came, *the law of the sin offering* could temporarily protect sinners from *the law of sin and death*.
     (Hint: these two terms are explained in Episode 5.)

B   The system of offering animal blood for the forgiveness of sins was only a picture of what God really required. Fill in the blanks using the words from the box below.

The **sacrifices** under the old system were repeated _____, year after year, but they were never able to provide _____ for those who came to worship. If they could have provided perfect cleansing, the sacrifices would have stopped, for the worshipers would have been _____ once for _____, and their feelings of guilt would have disappeared. But just the opposite happened. Those yearly sacrifices reminded them of their sins year after year. For it is not possible for the blood of _____ to take away _____ (Hebrews 10:1-4 NLT).

> perfect cleansing • ~~sacrifices~~ • sins • again and again
> purified • all time • bulls and goats

C   Why was it not possible for animal sacrifices to take away the sin-debt of humans? (Hint: Are lambs and humans equal in value?)

36 MORE PROPHECIES

The Ten Commandments taught us that no matter how good we think we are, we are not good enough to live with God in heaven. We need a Savior. As the time for the Savior's arrival got closer and closer, the LORD told His prophets to write many more prophecies about this Messiah-King.

A **Write on the scroll some of the prophecies about the coming Savior** (See Psalm 22:16, Isaiah 7:14, 9:6, 35:4-6 and 53:7; Micah 5:2). **Then choose one prophecy from the scroll and tell how you think it pointed to Him.**

8

Part 2

THE KING FULFILLS HIS PLAN

— NEW TESTAMENT —

EPISODE 9
THE KING'S ENTRANCE

KING of GLORY • SCENES 37–42

INTRODUCE

In the previous episode we completed our panoramic journey through the first part of the King's Book, the Old Testament. For thousands of years, using many pictures (such as sacrificed sheep) and prophecies, God announced His plan to send to earth the mighty Savior, who would defeat the law of sin and death and open the door to eternal life.

In today's episode, we will hear these words:

It was time. After thousands of years of preparation, God was about to send the promised Savior-Messiah-King into the world. But who would He be? And how would He come?

These questions and many more will be answered as we continue our journey into the New Testament Scriptures.

Like a seed that sprouts and grows into a mature tree, so God's plan for mankind takes root in the Old Testament and comes to completion in the New Testament.

It is time for the second stage of our journey.

It is time to discover that what the King *foretold* through His prophets, He has *fulfilled*.

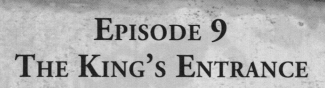

WATCH (⏱20:16)

Episode 9 covers **Scenes 37–42**

DISCUSS

1. What did you like about this episode?

2. What did you notice about God's character in this episode?

3. What kinds of jobs did angels perform in these stories? How do you think you would respond if an angel appeared to you?

4. Tell about some events surrounding Jesus' birth that made it like no other.

5. In this episode, we heard the angel Gabriel call Jesus *the Son of God*. What does this term mean? What does it *not* mean?

6. Who were the first people to hear the news that Jesus had been born? How did they respond?

7. What did the Magi do when they saw the little boy Jesus? Were they right or wrong to worship Him? Explain.

REFLECT

In the beginning was the Word, and the Word was with God, and the Word was God. He was with God in the beginning. Through him all things were made; without him nothing was made that has been made. … The Word became flesh and made his dwelling among us. We have seen his glory, the glory of the one and only Son, who came from the Father, full of grace and truth. (John 1:1-3,14)

REINFORCE

Review Episode 9 by doing the activities on the following pages.

37 THE KING'S STORY CONTINUES

📖 MATTHEW 1

A Mark the following statements true or false.

1. Testament means *agreement* or *covenant*.   True   False

2. Both *"Gospel"* and *"Injil"* (Arabic word) mean *Good News*.   True   False

3. The new covenant is not mentioned in the Old Testament.   True   False

4. God chose Matthew, Mark, Luke, and John to write   True   False
   four separate reports about the Messiah's life.

B Fill in the blanks with words from the box below.

In the _____ with His people, God gave them many
_____ to show them His _____ and their
_____. He also gave them many pictures and
_____ about the coming Savior. In the old covenant
the prophets foretold: "The Messiah-King _____." But in
the new covenant we read: "The Messiah-King _____!"

> **has come · sinfulness · first covenant · laws**
> **prophecies · will come · holiness**

C Answer the following questions.

1. The New Testament registers an unbroken chain of descendants from
   Abraham to Jesus. What does this teach us about God?

   _____
   _____

2. The New Testament contains four gospel books. Why not just one?
   (Hint: see Deuteronomy 19:15.)

   _____
   _____

This very old (3ʳᵈ or 4ᵗʰ century) papyrus*
is a page from the Gospel of Matthew.
The New Testament Scriptures are the best preserved
of all ancient writings. Nearly 25,000 handwritten copies
of the Bible have been discovered, of which 5,600 are
copies and fragments in the original Greek.
These manuscripts show that the Bible we have today
tells the same story and message as the originals.
God has preserved His truth for every generation.

*Papyrus (pictured) is a plant that grows wild all over the Nile
River Valley in Egypt from which a kind of paper is made.

38 MARY'S STORY

📖 LUKE 1

A Connect the names with the information about each person. Some names connect to more than one piece of information.

1. Herod
2. Gabriel
3. Joseph
4. Mary
5. Jesus

a. Son of the Most High God
b. an angel
c. the Word and Son of God
d. a young woman
e. a descendant of David
f. the fiancé of Mary
g. King of Judea
h. son of Mary
i. a virgin
j. One whose kingdom will never end

B Why did Gabriel tell Mary that her son would be called "the Son of God"? Mark the following reasons as true or false.

1. Because God planned to take Mary as His wife and father a son.   True   False

2. Because Mary's son would come from God and not from man.   True   False

3. Because her son would enter the human family as the promised *"Offspring of the woman"* (Genesis 3:15).   True   False

4. Because Gabriel wanted to blaspheme God.   True   False

5. Because the prophet Isaiah had written, *"The virgin will conceive a child! She will give birth to a son and will call him Immanuel"* (Isaiah 7:14 NLT).   True   False

6. Because in the Psalms, the prophet David refers to the Messiah as God's Son (Psalm 2).   True   False

7. Because Gabriel believed in more than one god.   True   False

8. Because this *"Holy One"* (Luke 1:35) would be born with God's perfect nature. Like Father, like Son.   True   False

9. Because Jesus is *"the Word [who] was with God in the beginning"* (John 1:2).   True   False

9

"So the Word became human …."
JOHN 1:14 NLT

C Answer the following questions.

1. From what you just heard from Scripture, tell something about the story of the angel coming to Mary. Why did the angel come to her? What did he tell her? How did Mary respond?

_____

_____

_____

_____

_____

2. On the day Adam ate the forbidden fruit, God made a promise. What was that ancient promise? And what did it have to do with Mary?

    a. That a baby named Jesus would come to destroy the Roman army that oppressed Mary.

    b. That the Offspring of a woman would crush the Serpent's head. That promised Offspring was now in Mary's womb!

39 JOSEPH'S STORY

📖 MATTHEW 1

A **Each picture and description represents an event that happened in Joseph's life. In the white box, use the numbers 1-4 to order the events chronologically.**

a. Joseph learned the shocking news: Mary was pregnant. Joseph was heartbroken, because it appeared that Mary had been unfaithful to him. He decided to break the engagement discreetly.

b. Joseph pledged to marry Mary. Both Mary and Joseph were Jews, tracing their ancestry to King David and on back to Abraham.

c. Joseph brought Mary home to be his wife, but she remained a virgin until her son was born. And Joseph named him Jesus.

d. An angel of the Lord appeared to Joseph in a dream and said, "Do not be afraid to go ahead with your marriage to Mary. For the child within her has been conceived by the Holy Spirit."

B **Mark the following statements true or false.**

1. Joseph was a carpenter by trade. — True — False

2. When Joseph learned that Mary was pregnant he arranged to have her flogged with 100 lashes. — True — False

3. The angel told Joseph to name Mary's son *Jesus*. — True — False

4. The name Jesus means *God is with us*. — True — False

5. The coming of the Savior fulfilled events the prophets had foretold long beforehand. — True — False

6. Mary would be the mother of the promised Messiah. — True — False

"Joseph, son of David," the angel said, "do not be afraid to go ahead with your marriage to Mary. For the child within her has been conceived by the Holy Spirit. And she will have a son, and you are to name him Jesus, for he will save his people from their sins."
MATTHEW 1:20-21 NLT

9

40 THE ARRIVAL

📖 LUKE 2

A Write the names of the two towns mentioned in this scene.

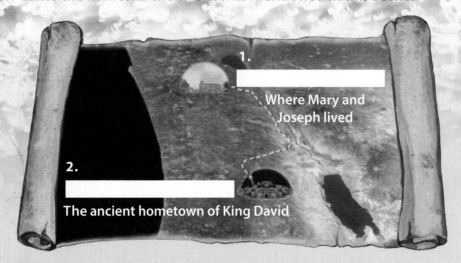

1.

Where Mary and
Joseph lived

2.

The ancient hometown of King David

B Answer the following questions.

1. How did God work it out so that Mary and Joseph were in Bethlehem
    for the Messiah's birth (as prophesied)?

2. Where was the King of heaven born?
    a. a royal palace   b. a barn
    c. a hospital   d. an inn

3. On His mother's side, Jesus was the newborn son of Mary.
    On His Father's side, He was:
    a. the eternal Son of God.   b. the newborn son of Joseph

The hills of Bethlehem today, where the
heavenly host appeared to shepherds.

41 THE SHEPHERDS' STORY

📖 LUKE 2

A   Answer the following questions.

1. To whom did God first make known the news of the Messiah's arrival?

   a. to the emperor
   b. to the religious leaders
   c. to the rich and famous
   d. to poor shepherds

2. How did God reveal the glorious news?

3. How did the people who hear the good news respond to it?

But the angel said to them,
"Do not be afraid.
I bring you good news of great joy
that will be for all the people.
Today in the town of David
a Savior has been born to you;
he is Christ the Lord!"
LUKE 2:10-11

9

42 THE MAGI'S STORY

📖 MATTHEW 2

A Answer the following questions.

1. One day some travel-weary but excited Magi (wise men) arrived in Jerusalem. Who or what were they searching for?
   a. riches
   b. a newborn King
   c. a prophet
   d. adventure

2. How did the Magi find out about the newborn King?
   a. They had received a letter from King Herod.
   b. They had seen His star in the East and had come to worship Him.

3. King Herod asked the teachers of the law in Jerusalem where the Messiah was to be born. How did they know the answer?
   a. Hundreds of years earlier, one of God's prophets had written that He would be born in Bethlehem.
   b. They checked the birth registry in Bethlehem.

4. What directed the Magi to the place where the child was?

5. How did the Magi respond when they saw the child Jesus with his mother? Was this a right response? Why or why not?

6. Which was *not* one of the gifts brought to Jesus?
   a. a camel train
   b. a spice for embalming the dead
   c. incense
   d. gold

All of this happened to fulfill the
Lord's message through his prophet:
"Look! The virgin will conceive a child!
She will give birth to a son,
and he will be called Immanuel
(meaning, God is with us)."

MATTHEW 1:22-23

9

Episode 10
The King's Character
KING of GLORY • SCENES 43–47

Introduce

The story is told of two men who, one dark night, fell into a deep, muddy well. Both lay at the bottom, injured. In the darkness, one cried out to the other, "Save me from this pit!" The other groaned, "I can't save you. I'm in the same mess!" Later, they heard a voice from above. A rescuer was lowered into the well. Their lives were spared. Only someone from outside the pit could rescue them.

Likewise, not even the best of the prophets could save us from the pit of sin. Like you and me, they too came from Adam's family, and were born with a sin nature. But the Messiah did not inherit that sinful nature. He was born with a holy nature. He came from above.

Do you remember what the prophet Isaiah had foretold? He prophesied that a virgin would become pregnant and give birth to a sinless son, and that He would be called *Immanuel*, which means, *God With Us* (Isaiah 7:14; 9:6; Matthew 1:23).

Our sin separates us from our holy God. But the Scripture says that *the Messiah "came into the world to save sinners"* (1 Timothy 1:15). He came to rescue us from the pit of sin.

Adam, the first man, led the human race far away from God. But Jesus the Messiah came to bring us back to God.

It is time to meet the perfect Man.

WATCH (🕐15:32)

Episode 10 covers **Scenes 43–47**

DISCUSS

1. What did you notice in this episode about the character of God? What did you notice about the character of Jesus?

2. How was the boy Jesus similar to other children, and how was He different?

3. Tell what you know about the prophet John. Which prophecies did he fulfill?

4. Why did people come to John to be baptized?

5. Why did the prophet John call Jesus "the Lamb of God"?

6. What is the big difference between lambs offered on altars in Old Testament times, and the sacrifice that the Lamb of God came to make? (Hint: see John 1:29 below.)

7. How was the oneness of God revealed at the baptism of Jesus? (Hint: His three-in-one, complex oneness.)

8. When the devil confronted Jesus in the desert, what was the devil trying to do? How did Jesus respond?

9. Name some ways that Jesus was different from Adam.

10. After Jesus read from the scroll of the prophet Isaiah, He said, "Today this scripture is fulfilled in your hearing." How did His neighbors react and why?

10

REFLECT

The next day John saw Jesus coming toward him and said,
"Look, the Lamb of God, who takes away
the sin of the world!" (John 1:29)

REINFORCE

Review Episode 10 by doing the activities on the following pages.

The Jordan River flows through the Sea of Galilee and ends in the Dead Sea.

43 THE PERFECT CHILD

📖 LUKE 2

A Answer the following questions.

1. Name some ways in which Jesus was *similar to* other children.

2. Name some ways in which Jesus was *different from* other children.

3. When Jesus was 12 years old He traveled with His parents from Nazareth to Jerusalem. Where did Jesus spend His time? What was He doing? How did the scholars react to Him?

4. Jesus was in Jerusalem at the time of the annual Feast of the Sacrifice, known as the Passover. Lambs were burned on an altar for the sins of the people. What did Jesus understand that the scholars did not?

B Mark the following statements true or false.

1. Jesus was the only perfect child in history.   True   False

2. When the Bible says that Jesus was perfect, it means that He never had a skinned knee or a pimple.   True   False

3. Even as a boy, Jesus had a special understanding of God's law.   True   False

He was holy, blameless, pure, set apart from sinners. HEBREWS 7:26

Jesus grew in wisdom and stature, and in favor with God and man. LUKE 2:52

44 THE LAMB OF GOD

📖 MATTHEW 3, JOHN 1

Thirty years after Jesus' birth in Bethlehem, a new prophet named John the Baptist was preaching in Palestine. He was the King's forerunner.

A Answer the following questions.

1. The previous prophets had foretold: *At the right time, the promised Savior will come to earth.* How was the prophet John's message different?

    _____

    _____

    _____

2. Crowds came to the desert to hear John. What did John do to those who confessed their condition as sinners in need of the Savior?

    a. John baptized them.   b. John forgave their sins.

    c. John washed their feet.   d. John healed them.

B Fill in the blanks with the words from the box below.

1. John declared, " *Repent* , for the _____ of heaven is near."

2. John was the one spoken of by the prophet Isaiah. He said that John would come saying, "_____ the way for the _____ , make straight paths for him."

3. John's _____ were made of camel's hair, and he had a leather belt round his waist. His food was _____ and wild honey.

4. John pointed to Jesus and said, "Look, the _____ of God, who takes away the sin of the world!"

> ~~repent~~ • kingdom • prepare • Lamb • Lord • clothes • locusts

10

C Answer the following questions.

1. From what we learned in the Old Testament Scriptures, we know that ever since sin came into the human family, the blood of the animal sacrifices which God required could only *cover sin* for a limited time. Why do you think the prophet John called Jesus "the Lamb of God, who *takes away the sin of the world*"?

_____
_____
_____
_____

2. Using your hand to represent the blood of sacrificed animals, cover the dirty heart below and explain what the blood of animals **could** and **could not** do. (Hint: see Hebrews 10:1-14.)

John pointed to Jesus and said,
"Look, the Lamb of God,
who takes away the sin of the world!"
JOHN 1:29

45 THE PERFECT SON

A   Tell about what you see in this picture.

B   God's (three-in-one) unity is again revealed in this event. Connect the names on the left to the phrases on the right that best match them. Each name will connect to two phrases.

a.   came upon the Son in the form of a dove

1.   The Spirit of God

b.   spoke from heaven at Jesus' baptism

c.   hovered over the waters in the beginning

2.   The Son of God

d.   was baptized by John

e.   "the Word" who created the world in the beginning

3.   The Father

f.   observed every thought, word, and action of the Son and gave His verdict at Jesus' baptism

C Answer the following questions.

1. The voice from heaven said, *"This is my Son, whom I love; with him I am well pleased!"* (Matthew 3:17) What was the Father saying about the Son?

   a. The Father was saying that the Son was His favorite prophet.

   b. The Father was saying that the Son was His sinless and perfect Word who was representing Him on earth.

2. What do you think Jesus meant when He said, *"I and the Father are one"*?

   a. That Jesus was merely a great prophet who spoke for God.

   b. That Jesus was one with God, the Word of God who created the world.

3. Based on the biblical record of Jesus' baptism, what made Jesus different from any other human in history?

   a. Jesus was a *great* carpenter.

   b. Jesus spent time with *people*.

   c. Jesus was baptized in *water*.

   d. Jesus *always* pleased God.

10

In the past God spoke to our ancestors through the prophets at many times and in various ways, but in these last days he has spoken to us by his Son, whom he appointed heir of all things, and through whom also he made the universe. The Son is the radiance of God's glory and the exact representation of his being, sustaining all things by his powerful word!
HEBREWS 1:1-3A

46 THE SECOND MAN

📖 MATTHEW 4

A Mark the following statements true or false.

1. Satan was happy that the Messiah had come to live in his kingdom! — True (False)

2. Just as he had tempted the first man to sin, so now the devil would try to get this Man to sin. — True False

3. Satan wanted to bring Jesus under his control. — True False

4. If the Son of God could be enticed to sin, then He would not be qualified to save His people from their sin. — True False

5. Jesus had been fasting for thirty days and thirty nights. — True False

6. Jesus was so hungry that He turned the stones to bread. — True False

7. Jesus combatted Satan by quoting from the Torah of Moses. — True False

8. Jesus did not sin. — True False

9. Satan had never tempted anyone like Jesus. Jesus was different from Adam and his descendants. — True False

Jesus said to him, "Away from me, Satan! For it is written: 'Worship the Lord your God, and serve him only.'" MATTHEW 4:10

B Compare Adam and Jesus by filling in the blanks with the words from the box below. Each word should only be used once.

1. "The first man was of the dust of the <u>earth</u>, the second man from _____" (1 Corinthians 15:47).

2. Adam was the first _____ man.
   Jesus was the second _____ man.

3. When Satan tempted Adam to sin, _____ lost and _____ won. When Satan tried to get Jesus to sin, _____ lost and _____ won.

4. The first man led us _____ Satan's kingdom of sin and death. The Second Man came to lead us _____.

10

Satan • heaven • perfect • Satan • Adam
~~earth~~ • Jesus • into • out • perfect

47 THE MESSIAH KING

📖 LUKE 4

A Connect the words and their descriptions.

1. Nazareth

2. synagogue

3. Isaiah

4. scroll

a. a house of worship where the Scriptures were read and explained every Saturday

b. an ancient kind of book that can be rolled up

c. the town where Jesus grew up

d. a prophet who had written about Jesus 700 years earlier

B Fill in the blanks with the words from the box below.

"The _____ is on me, because he has anointed me to preach _____ to the poor. He has sent me to proclaim freedom for the prisoners and recovery of sight for the _____ ...."

Then [Jesus] rolled up the _____, gave it back to the attendant and sat down. The eyes of everyone in the synagogue were fastened on him, and he began by saying to them, "_____, this scripture is _____ in your hearing!" (Luke 4:17-18, 20-21).

scroll • good news • Spirit of the Lord • blind • fulfilled • today

C Answer the following questions.

1. What did the verses Jesus read in the Scriptures (above) say about the Messiah-King and what He would do?

2. Jesus claimed to be the Messiah who came from heaven to fulfill the Scriptures of the prophets. How did His neighbors react to this claim?

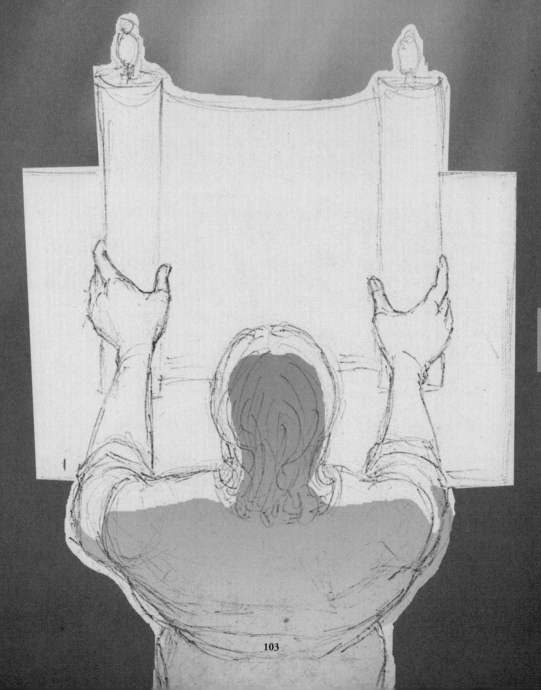

"Do not think that I have come to abolish the Law or the Prophets; I have not come to abolish them but to fulfill them."

MATTHEW 5:17

10

EPISODE 11
THE KING'S DOMINION

KING of GLORY • SCENES 48–51

INTRODUCE

If you want to get to know someone well, which is best: to communicate through letters and text messages, or to spend time together in person? The LORD God, who once walked and talked with Adam and Eve, never intended to limit His communication to words in a book. He planned to reveal Himself in person.

From the beginning, it was God's plan to take on a human body, to hunger and hurt, to experience our joys and pains, and then to fulfill His mission. Some people say that God is "too great" to do such a thing. But never in history did our Creator despise the idea of coming down to our level so that He could bring us up to His.

Living in the world He had made was part of our Creator-King's plan to save sinners from the law of sin and death, and bring us back to Himself. That is why Jesus told His disciples, *"the Son of Man came to seek and save those who are lost"* (Luke 19:10 NLT).

As you watch this next episode, think about how you would answer the question Jesus sometimes asked people:

"Who do YOU say I am?" (Mark 8:29).

WATCH (🕐14:02)

Episode 11 covers **Scenes 48–51**

DISCUSS

1. What surprised you in this episode?

2. How did Jesus demonstrate His power over nature?

3. What did Jesus see as the greatest need of people who were sick, blind, or paralyzed?

4. Why did the religious leaders accuse Jesus of blasphemy?

5. What did Jesus mean when He said, *"I am the resurrection and the life"*? How did He prove that His words were true?

6. Think about one of Jesus' miracles that is especially meaningful to you. Would you like to tell why?

7. Based on what you have seen and heard so far, who do you believe that Jesus is? Explain.

8. In what way did Jesus' miracles prove that His words were true? (Hint: John 11:25 + calling Lazarus out of the tomb.)

REFLECT

The disciples were absolutely terrified. "Who is this man?" they asked each other. "Even the wind and waves obey him!" (Mark 4:41)

Jesus said, "The time has come. The kingdom of God has come near. Repent and believe the good news!" (Mark 1:15)

REINFORCE

Review Episode 11 by doing the activities on the following pages.

11

48 DOMINION OVER DEMONS AND DISEASE

📖 LUKE 4

A Jesus did miracles while He was on earth. Circle the miracles that the Scriptures say Jesus did.

made the blind see • made the lame walk • cured leprosy

made poor people wealthy • made the deaf hear • raised the dead

B Answer the following questions.

1. How did Jesus' ability to do miracles prove His claim to be the Messiah?

2. How did the demons know who Jesus was? Explain.

3. What did the demons shout when Jesus cast them out?

   a. "You are the Son of God!"   c. "Have mercy on us!"

   b. "Release us from our torment."   d. "Who are you?"

4. What was happening to Satan's power and dominion over the earth as the King of glory invaded Satan's domain?

C Mark the following statements true or false.

1. "The Arm of the LORD" was one of the Messiah's titles.   True   False

2. Jesus could heal only some kinds of diseases.   True   False

3. The demons knew who Jesus was and were afraid of Him.   True   False

4. Jesus' message was "The kingdom of God has come near. Repent and believe the good news!"   True   False

The Sea of Galilee today. At 215 metres below sea level, it is the lowest freshwater lake on Earth.

49 DOMINION OVER WIND AND WAVES

📖 MARK 4

A Number the pictures so that they match the order of events.

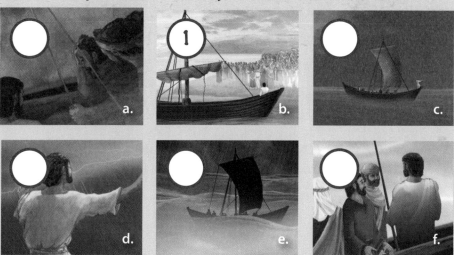

1. Jesus was teaching by the lakeshore. There was such a large crowd that He got into a boat and sat down and spoke from there.

2. After he finished teaching, Jesus told His disciples to sail to the other side of the lake. But soon a fierce storm came up. High waves were breaking into the boat, and it began to fill with water.

3. Jesus was sleeping at the back of the boat. The disciples woke him up, shouting, "Teacher, don't you care that we're going to drown?"

4. When Jesus woke up, He rebuked the wind and said to the waves, "Silence! Be still!"

5. Suddenly, the wind stopped, and there was a great calm.

6. Then he asked them, "Why are you afraid? Do you still have no faith?" The disciples were absolutely terrified. "Who is this man?" they asked each other. "Even the wind and waves obey him!"

11

"They were at their wits' end. Then they cried out to the LORD in their trouble, and he brought them out of their distress. He stilled the storm to a whisper; the waves of the sea were hushed."

—PROPHET DAVID (PSALM 107:27-29)

B Mark the following statements true or false.

1. Jesus selected twelve men to travel with Him and learn   True   False
    from Him. They were called "disciples."

2. Most of Jesus' disciples were carpenters.   True   False

3. There were no women who followed or supported Jesus.   True   False

4. Jesus' call was simple but costly.   True   False

5. Jesus said that people who love their family members   True   False
    more than they love Him are not worthy of Him.[3]

C Jesus could calm the wind and waves by simply speaking to them. What does this teach you about who Jesus is?

"Follow me."

"Anyone who loves his father or mother more than me
is not worthy of me; anyone who loves his son or daughter
more than me is not worthy of me."

—The Lord Jesus LUKE 5:27; MATTHEW 10:37

50 DOMINION OVER SIN

📖 MARK 2

A Answer the following questions.

1. One day, four men carrying a stretcher with a crippled man came to Jesus. What did Jesus say first to the paralyzed man?

   a. "Why have you come?"   b. "Your sins are forgiven."

   c. "Where is your faith?"   d. "Stand up and walk."

2. Jesus knew that this man's greatest need was

   a. to be forgiven of his sins.   b. to walk again.

3. The teachers of the religious law thought Jesus was blaspheming because

   a. they knew His thoughts.   b. only God can forgive sins.

4. How did Jesus know the religious teachers' thoughts?

   a. He was good at guessing.   b. He knows all things.

5. The Son of Man proved that He had authority on earth to forgive sins by

   a. forgiving the man's sins.   b. making the man able to walk.

6. How did the onlookers respond to the miracle?

   a. They were amazed and praised God.

   b. They asked the teachers of the law to rebuke Jesus.

   c. They did not notice the miracle.

7. What blinded the teachers from seeing who Jesus is? (Choose two answers.)

   a. their religion.   b. lack of sleep

   c. the room was dark.   d. their pride

8. Based on this story, what do you think these hearts symbolize? Explain.

9. Different people believed different things about Jesus. From what we have learned in the last two stories, who do *you* think Jesus is? Explain.

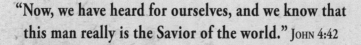

"Now, we have heard for ourselves, and we know that this man really is the Savior of the world." JOHN 4:42

11

51 DOMINION OVER DEATH

📖 LUKE 7; JOHN 11

A Answer the following questions.

1. Jesus had dominion over every part of creation. Yet He didn't go around saying, "Worship Me! I am God!" What did He do instead, and why?

   _____

   _____

   _____

2. The Bible says that when Jesus was in a town called Nain, he commanded a lady's dead son to get up out of his coffin. What happened? How did the people respond? (Choose two answers.)

   a. The dead man came back to life.

   b. The dead man remained in his coffin and was buried.

   c. The people sought to take Jesus' life.

   d. The people were all filled with awe and praised God.

3. In thinking through this episode's scenes (48-51), how many powerful things can you think of that Jesus had dominion (control) over?

   Jesus had dominion over demons and disease.

   Jesus had dominion over...

   _____

   _____

   _____

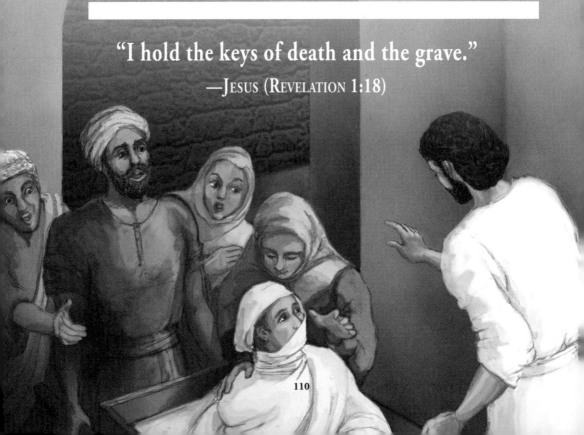

> ## "I hold the keys of death and the grave."
> —JESUS (REVELATION 1:18)

B Fill in the blanks in this conversation from John 11 with the words from the box below. Some words will be used more than once.

Martha : "If you had been here, my brother would not have **died** ."

_____ : "I am the _____ and the _____. He who believes in me will live, even though he dies; and whoever lives and believes in me will never die. Do you believe this?"

_____ : "Yes … I believe that you are the _____, the _____, who was to come into the world."

_____ : "Take away the _____."

_____ : "But … he has been there four days."

_____ : "Did I not tell you that if you _____, you would see the glory of _____? … Lazarus, come out! … Take off the grave clothes and let him go."

> Martha · Son of God · resurrection · God
> stone · died · Christ · believed · life · Jesus

C Jesus said, *"I AM the Resurrection and the Life"* (John 11:25). How could people know that His words were true?

_____
_____
_____
_____

11

EPISODE 12
THE KING'S MISSION
KING OF GLORY • SCENES 52–56

INTRODUCE

One of the Messiah's titles is *The Word of God*. Yes, He was and is the same Voice, who on the first day of creation said, "Let there be light," and there was light. He is the One who on the third day said, "Let dry ground appear." And that is what happened. It was also He who on the fifth day said, "Let the skies be filled with birds of every kind." And that is what happened.

That same Voice was now in a human body, living on earth among the human family He had come to rescue.

Do you remember what Jesus said to the religious leaders after He had told the lame man, *"My child, your sins are forgiven"*? He said to them, *"I will prove to you that the Son of Man has authority on earth to forgive sins." Then Jesus turned to the paralyzed man and said, "Stand up, pick up your mat, and go home!"* (Mark 2:5,10-11). And that is what happened.

Who can forgive sins but God? Jesus forgave sins. Who can open the eyes of the blind but God? Jesus opened blind eyes. Who can still the wind but God? Jesus stilled the wind and waves. Who can raise the dead to life but God? Jesus raised dead people.

But He had not come to earth just to show us what God is like. He came to make a way back to God.

It is time to learn more about His mission.

WATCH (⏱15:24)

Episode 12 covers **Scenes 52–56**

DISCUSS

1. Which of the teachings of Jesus stands out to you the most? Why?

2. What is a false prophet? Why did Jesus tell people to beware of them?

3. What made Jesus different from God's prophets who came before Him?

4. What did Jesus mean when He described Himself as
   a. *"the bread of life"*? (John 6:35)
   b. *"the way, and the truth, and the life"*? (John 14:6)
   c. *"the light of the world"*? (John 8:12)

5. What did the voice from heaven say about Jesus when He was transfigured on the mountain top?

6. What was the purpose of Jesus' coming? What did Jesus foretell would take place in Jerusalem to fulfill that purpose? How did Jesus know this would happen?

7. How did Jesus' entrance into Jerusalem fulfill a 500-year-old prophecy?

REFLECT

As Jesus was going up to Jerusalem, he took the twelve disciples aside privately and told them what was going to happen to him. "Listen," he said, "we're going up to Jerusalem, where the Son of Man will be betrayed to the leading priests and the teachers of religious law. They will sentence him to die. Then they will hand him over to the Romans to be mocked, flogged with a whip, and crucified. But on the third day he will be raised from the dead." (Matthew 20:17-20 NLT)

REINFORCE

Review Episode 12 by doing the activities on the following pages.

12

Fields near the Sea of Galilee, where Jesus often taught the crowds, and sometimes fed them.

52 THE PROVIDER

📖 JOHN 6

A Answer the following questions about Jesus the Provider.

1. How many people were gathered on the hillside on this particular day?

    a. more than 500   b. about 100

    c. about 1,000   d. more than 5,000

2. Jesus asked His disciples where they could buy bread to feed the people. Andrew found a young boy with food. What did he have?

    a. five loaves and two fish   b. two loaves and five fish

3. Tell about what Jesus did with the young boy's lunch.

    _____

    _____

    _____

4. On the next day, what did the crowd want to do with Jesus, and why?

    _____

    _____

    _____

5. Jesus told them that they should not be so concerned about perishable things like food. What should they spend their energy seeking?

    _____

    _____

    _____

6. What do you think Jesus meant when He said, "I AM the bread of life"?

    _____

    _____

Jesus said to them, "I am the bread of life. No one who comes to me will ever be hungry again. Those who believe in me will never thirst."
JOHN 6:35 NLT

53 THE TEACHER

📖 MATTHEW 5-7

Jesus was a different kind of teacher — He was the teacher from heaven.

A Answer the following questions about Jesus the Teacher.

1. How was Jesus different from the *religious teachers*?

2. How was Jesus different from the *prophets* who had come before Him?

B Match the questions people ask with the answers Jesus taught.

1. How should I treat
   my enemies?

2. How should I pray?

3. Is it OK to worry?

4. What is the most important
   thing in life?

5. What should I do about
   false prophets?

a. Seeking God's kingdom
   and His righteousness.

b. Pagans do this, but you can
   trust that your Heavenly
   Father knows your needs.

c. Love and pray for them.

d. Watch out for such "wolves
   in sheep's clothing" whose
   lies can destroy you.

e. Do this in private, not for
   others to see but for your
   Heavenly Father to see (to
   spend time with Him).

"I AM the way
and the truth
and the life."
JOHN 14:6

12

C Use the images below to retell Jesus' story about two houses (Matthew 7:24-27).

D If you hear and practice (believe and obey) Jesus' words, to what does He compare you? If you don't act on His words, to what does He compare you?

"Everyone who hears these words of mine
and puts them into practice
is like a wise man who built his house on the rock."
—Jesus MATTHEW 7:24

54 His Majesty

A Who said it? Match the phrases with the names.

1. "Why didn't you bring [Jesus] in?"　　　　　a. the temple guards

2. "No one ever spoke the way this man does."　　b. the chief priests

3. "I AM the light of the world."

　　　　　　　　　　　　　　　　　　　　　c. God the Father

4. "The Sun of Righteousness will rise… ."

　　　　　　　　　　　　　　　　　　　　　d. the prophet Malachi

5. "This is my Son, whom I love; with him
　 I am well pleased. Listen to him!"　　　　　e. Jesus, the Son of God

B Answer the following questions.

1. Why were the teachers and the priests of the Jews not happy to see the crowds listening to Jesus?

_____

_____

2. Jesus said, "I AM the light of the world. Whoever follows me will … have the light of life" (John 8:12). What did He mean by this?

   a. That He is the ultimate Source of physical and spiritual light.

   b. That His face always shines like the sun.

> **"We were eye-witnesses of his majesty!"**
> 2 PETER 1:16

55 HIS MISSION

📖 MATTHEW 16, 20

For three years, the Lord Jesus had been doing good and healing many people. But was there more to His mission than that?

A Answer the following questions.

1. Who loved Jesus?

    a. the religious leaders   b. the common people

2. Who hated Jesus and wanted to kill Him?

    a. the religious leaders   b. the common people

3. In the picture below, where is Jesus going?
    (Hint: He told His disciples that He must go there and suffer.)

    a. to Nazareth   b. to Jerusalem

    c. to Bethlehem   d. to Galilee

4. What did Peter say when Jesus told His disciples that He would be tortured, killed, and then rise again? What kind of Messiah did His disciples want?

    _____

    _____

    _____

5. The disciples had not yet understood Jesus' mission. What was Jesus' mission on His first coming to earth?

    _____

    _____

6. Jesus said, "Whoever wants to become great among you must be your _____, … just as the Son of Man did not come to be served, but to serve, and to give his life as a ransom for many" (Matthew 20:26,28).

    a. teacher   b. servant

    c. leader   d. king

56 THE KING ENTERS JERUSALEM

📖 MARK 11

A Fill in the blanks with words from the box below.

As he rode along, the crowds spread out their _____ on the road ahead of him. When he reached the place where the road started down the Mount of Olives, all of his followers began to _____ and sing as they walked along, praising God for all the wonderful _____ they had seen. "Blessings on the _____ who comes in the name of the _____! Peace in heaven, and _____ in highest heaven!" (Luke 19:30-38 NLT).

Lord · King · miracles · glory · garments · shout

B What had Jesus come to save people from?

a. from the Romans

b. from poverty and war

c. from their corrupt religious leaders

d. from their sins

The East Gate, also called The Golden Gate, is where Jesus entered Jerusalem on a donkey on His way to the cross. This gate is presently sealed shut, but the Scriptures foretell that when the Messiah returns to judge the world, He will enter Jerusalem once more through this gate.

12

EPISODE 13
THE KING'S SUBMISSION
KING OF GLORY • SCENES 57–61

INTRODUCE

In the last episode we heard Jesus the Messiah talk about His mission: why He had come from heaven to earth.

Do you remember what He said to His disciples as they were traveling to Jerusalem? Jesus told them that He was going there to suffer and die.

Do you know *where* you will die? Do you know *how* you will die? Or *when* you will die? We do not know these things. But Jesus was not like us. He knew *where* He would die and He announced it to His disciples (Matthew 16:21).

He also foretold *how* He would die. He would be arrested and condemned by the religious leaders, and then tortured and crucified by the Romans (Matthew 20:17-19).

Jesus also told His disciples *when* He would die. He would shed His blood on the same day the Jews were killing lambs to celebrate the feast of the Passover (Matthew 26:1-2).

Jesus also knew *why* He would die. He told His disciples, *"I am the good shepherd. The good shepherd lays down his life for the sheep"* (John 10:11).

It was time for the King of glory to lay down His life.

WATCH (🕐14:50)

Episode 13 covers **Scenes 57–61**

DISCUSS

1. Why didn't the religious leaders want Jesus to be king?

2. What did Jesus give the disciples to eat and drink at their last meal together? What did the food and drink represent?

3. Why did Jesus not defend Himself when the soldiers came to arrest Him? What was the religious leaders' accusation against Him?

4. Name some similarities between Abraham's offering on Mount Moriah (Episode 7) and God's offering on the same mountain range.

5. Name some Old Testament prophecies that were fulfilled when Jesus was crucified.

6. From a human perspective, why was Jesus crucified even though He was innocent? From God's perspective, why was Jesus crucified?

7. What was the price that God paid to ransom you?

8. How much are you worth to God?

REFLECT

God paid a ransom to save you from the empty life you inherited from your ancestors. And the ransom he paid was not mere gold or silver. He paid for you with the precious lifeblood of Christ, the sinless, spotless Lamb of God. (1 Peter 1:18-19 NLT)

REINFORCE

Review Episode 13 by doing the activities on the following pages.

13

This rocky hill is part of the mountain range that the prophet Abraham named *The LORD Will Provide.*
This mountain has several other names: *Golgotha*, *The Place of the Skull*, and *Calvary*.

57 THE KING IS QUESTIONED

📖 LUKE 20

A Mark the following statements about the temple leaders true or false.

1. The temple leaders encouraged the common people to follow Jesus.   True (False)

2. The temple leaders wanted Jesus to be their King.   True False

3. The temple leaders sent spies to try to get Jesus to say something that could get Him arrested.   True False

4. The temple leaders trapped Jesus with their questions.   True False

B Answer the following questions.

1. How did the leaders of the temple respond when, as a boy, Jesus asked deep questions and gave wise answers in the temple? How had their attitude toward Jesus changed?

_____

_____

_____

2. Jesus was asked, "Is it right for us to pay taxes to Caesar or not?" (Luke 20:22 NLT). Was this a trick question? If so, in what way? What was Jesus' response?

_____

_____

_____

_____

3. How did the people react to Jesus' answer? What did Jesus' enemies do next?

_____

_____

58 THE KING IS ARRESTED

📖 MARK 14

A From the event of Jesus' last supper with His disciples, tell about the items on the right. What are they and what do they represent?

B Connect the words with the phrases that best match them.

1. Passover   a. a title Jesus often used in speaking of Himself

2. lambs   b. the annual Feast of Sacrifice

3. torn bread   c. a reminder of Jesus' blood

4. cup of juice   d. a garden where Jesus prayed to his Father

5. Gethsemane   e. a reminder of Jesus' body

6. the Son of Man   f. another name for God the Father

7. the Mighty One   g. thousands of these were killed at Passover

C What happened in the garden called Gethsemane?

Looking across the Kidron Valley towards Jerusalem's East Gate, this view is from the garden of Gethsemane, where Jesus let the soldiers arrest Him, bind Him, and lead Him to the chief religious leader's house to be judged and condemned.

13

D Answer the following questions about Jesus' arrest.

1. Whom did the religious leaders bring with them to arrest Jesus?

   a. a mob of armed men   b. a group of common people

2. Why did Jesus say the arrest was happening?

   a. to perform justice   b. to fulfill the words of the prophets

3. What did the disciples do when Jesus was arrested?

   a. they fled   b. they prayed for Him

E Fill in the blanks using the words from the box below.

Then the   **high priest**   stood up before them and asked Jesus,
"Are you not going to answer? What is this _____ that these
men are bringing against you?" But Jesus remained _____
and gave no answer. Again the high priest asked him, "Are you the
_____, the Son of the Blessed One?"

"_____," said Jesus. "And you will see the Son of Man sitting
at the right hand of the Mighty One and coming on the clouds of heaven."

The high priest tore his clothes. "Why do we need any more witnesses?"
he asked. "You have heard the _____. What do you think?"

They all condemned him as worthy of _____.

Then some began to spit at him; they blindfolded him, struck him with
their fists, and said, "_____!" And the guards took him and
_____ him (Mark 14:56,60-65).

> death • Christ • Prophesy • testimony • silent
> ~~high priest~~ • I am • beat • blasphemy

59 THE KING IS CONDEMNED

📖 JOHN 18

A Match the correct letter with each picture.

a. Religious leaders   b. Pilate   c. Jesus   d. The mob

1.   2.   3.   4.

B Who said what? Fill in the names in this conversation.
Use the names from Question A, above.

_____ : "This man has been leading our people to ruin by telling them not to pay their taxes to the Roman government and by claiming he is the Messiah, a king."

_____ : "I find nothing wrong with this man!"

_____ : "If he were not a criminal, we would not have handed him over to you."

_____ : "Are you the king of the Jews? … What is it you have done?"

_____ : "My kingdom is not of this world. If it were, my servants would fight to prevent my arrest by the Jews. But my kingdom is from another place."

_____ : "You are a king, then!"

_____ : "You are right in saying I am a king. In fact, for this reason I was born, and for this I came into the world, to testify to the truth. Everyone on the side of truth listens to me."

_____ : "What is truth?"

_____ : "I find no basis for a charge against him."

_____ : "Crucify him! Crucify him!"

_____ : "Why? What crime has this man committed? I have found in him no grounds for the death penalty. Therefore I will have him punished and… release him."

But with loud shouts they insistently demanded that he be crucified, and their shouts prevailed (John 18:30, 33, 35-38; Luke 23:21-22).

13

C Answer the following questions.

1. In this scene, who lied, and what did they lie about?
   - (a.) The religious leaders, saying that Jesus was a criminal.
   - b. Jesus, saying that He was the King who came into the world to testify to the truth.

2. In this scene, who did *not* lie?
   - a. Jesus, when he said, "Everyone on the side of truth listens to me."
   - b. The religious leaders, when they said that Jesus "has been leading our people to ruin."

3. In the end, Pilate condemned Jesus to death. Why?
   - a. Because Pilate believed that Jesus was guilty.
   - b. Because Pilate was afraid of the religious leaders and their mob.

4. What did Jesus mean when He said that He was a king, but that his kingdom is *"not of this world"* and *"from another place"*?

   _____

   _____

   _____

Pilate said to the crowd:
"I find nothing wrong with this man!"
LUKE 23:4 NLT

60 THE KING IS CROWNED

📖 MATTHEW 27

A **Pilate sentenced Jesus to death by crucifixion. What happened before that? Circle the words that tell how Jesus was treated.**

whipped • beaten • stoned

mocked • spit upon • stripped

B **Answer the following questions.**

1. *"I offered my back to those who beat me, my cheeks to those who pulled out my beard; I did not hide my face from mocking and spitting."*
   When were these words of the Messiah written in the Scriptures?
   a. 700 years *before* Jesus was tortured by the soldiers
   b. 25 years *after* Jesus was tortured by the soldiers

2. Fill in the missing words from the prophecy of Abraham 1,900 years earlier. *"God himself will provide the _____ for the burnt offering."*
   a. ram   b. lamb

3. From which area of the world did the man come, who was forced to carry Jesus' cross?
   a. Europe   b. North Africa

4. What kind of crown was put on Jesus' head? What Old Testament story does this remind you of? Explain.

5. To which hill was Jesus taken to be crucified? What Old Testament story does this remind you of? Explain.

13

61 The King is Crucified

📖 LUKE 23

A Answer the following questions.

1. About 1,000 years before Jesus was crucified, the prophet King David wrote this about the Messiah:

   "They have pierced my hands and my feet. ... People stare and gloat over me. They divide my garments among them and cast lots for my clothing."
   " All who see me mock me; they hurl insults, shaking their heads:
   '... Let the LORD rescue him. Let him deliver him, since he delights in him!'"
   (Psalm 22:16-18, 6-8).

   Everything David foretold was fulfilled. For example, as prophesied, the religious leaders who watched Jesus' crucifixion said, "He saved others; let him save himself" (Matthew 27:42). But what would have happened if Jesus had saved Himself? **(Circle all that are true.)**

   a. He would not have fulfilled the Scriptures of the prophets.

   b. He could not have saved us.

   c. He would have failed in His mission.

2. About 1,900 years before the crucifixion of Jesus, the prophet Abraham told his son, *"God himself will provide the lamb for the burnt offering ... "* (Genesis 22:8). After God provided a ram as the substitute, Abraham named the mountain, *"The LORD Will Provide"* (Genesis 22:14). How did Jesus the Lamb of God (John 1:29) fulfill Abraham's prophecies?

   _____

   _____

   _____

So Abraham called that place *The LORD Will Provide.*
And to this day it is said, "On the mountain of the LORD it will be provided."
GENESIS 22:14

About 1900 BC

3. From what you have learned in the Old and New Testament Scriptures, explain how the two images on the right are similar yet different.

4. See if you can figure out what this timeline means. We'll come back to it in the next Episode.

Old Testament   New Testament

5. Do you think God loves you personally? Why do you think this?

For God so loved the world
that He gave His only begotten Son,
that whoever believes in Him
should not perish but have everlasting life.

JOHN 3:16 NKJV

13

About AD 30

EPISODE 14
THE KING'S SACRIFICE & TRIUMPH

KING OF GLORY • SCENES 62–65

INTRODUCE

What do you think about the Messiah's willingness to suffer and die for you—in your place, for your sins—and to endure the penalty you deserve?

Some people say, "God would never allow a great prophet like Jesus to suffer the pain and shame of crucifixion!" They say this because they have not yet grasped God's rescue plan, the repulsiveness of their sin, the fiery holiness of God, and the extravagance of God's amazing love.

Jesus said, *"I lay down my life—only to take it up again. No one takes it from me, but I lay it down of my own accord. I have authority to lay it down and authority to take it up again. This command I received from my Father"* (John 10:17-18).

Jesus knew why He had come into the world. He had come to endure the eternal punishment for sin in our place. He had come to bear the wrath of God because of our sin. He had come to rescue us from Satan, sin, death, and hell—and to bring us into a close and happy relationship with Himself forever.

Let's continue now with the most important part of the King's story and message.

WATCH (🕐13:53)

Episode 14 covers **Scenes 62–65**

DISCUSS

1. What touched you the most in this episode?

2. Concerning God's plan to rescue us from Satan, sin, death, and hell, the Scripture says, "*None of the rulers of this age understood it, for if they had, they would not have crucified the Lord of glory*" (1 Corinthians 2:8). Do *you* understand God's rescue plan? Explain.

3. Why is one of the criminals (who hung on the cross next to Jesus) in heaven today? Why is the other in hell?

4. As the Lord Jesus was suspended on the cross in the darkness, what did God in heaven load on Him?

5. How was Jesus' cross like an altar on which lambs were sacrificed?

6. Why did Jesus say, "My God, My God, why have you forsaken me?"

7. What did Jesus mean when He said, "It is finished"?

8. Did the disciples remember Jesus' promise to rise again? Did the religious leaders who condemned Jesus remember it?

9. What did the women find at the tomb early Sunday morning?

10. If I trust in the Lord Jesus as *my* Lamb, why do I need not fear death?

REFLECT

Who has believed our message? … All of us, like sheep, have strayed away. We have left God's paths to follow our own. Yet the LORD laid on HIM the sins of us all. (Isaiah 53:1a,6 NLT)

REINFORCE

Review Episode 14 by doing the activities on the following pages.

14

62 THE SAVIOR-KING

📖 LUKE 23

A **How do Jesus' sufferings connect to what happened to Adam and Eve? Match the words with the pictures.**

a.

1. Jesus felt the shame sin brings.

b.

2. Jesus was cursed in our place.

c.

3. Jesus took the punishment we deserve.

B **Answer the following questions.**

1. On the day Adam broke God's law, God had told Satan,
   "He will crush your head, and you will strike his heel" (Genesis 3:15).
   How did Satan strike Jesus' heel at the crucifixion?

_____

_____

_____

2. Were the people who crucified Jesus aware of God's secret plan to provide salvation for the world? How do you know this?

_____

_____

_____

> We declare God's wisdom, a mystery that has been hidden and
> that God destined for our glory before time began.
> None of the rulers of this age understood it, for if they had,
> they would not have crucified the Lord of glory.
> 1 CORINTHIANS 2:7-8

C **Jesus was crucified beside two criminals. Mark the following statements true or false.**

1. Both criminals spoke to Jesus while on the cross.   True   False

2. One of the criminals didn't deserve to be on the cross.   True   False

3. Both criminals were sinners.   True   False

4. Jesus said to both criminals, "I tell you the truth,   True   False
   today you will be with me in paradise."

5. One criminal went to hell to be forever
   separated from God.   True   False

6. One criminal went to paradise to be with Jesus.   True   False

History records the crucifixion of tens of thousands of people by the Roman Empire. In 1968, construction workers in East Jerusalem uncovered an ancient ossuary (bone box) in which was found this heel bone of a crucified victim. It reveals that the Roman soldiers hammered the nails through the man's heels and into the side of the cross (as portrayed in the *KING OF GLORY* movie and book). Jesus willingly suffered and died in this way to shed His blood for the sin of the world and *"to fulfill the words of the prophets as recorded in the Scriptures"* (Matthew 26:56 NLT).

14

63 THE FINAL SACRIFICE

📖 MATTHEW 27; JOHN 19

A From what you have learned about the purpose of Jesus' sufferings and death on the cross, tell about what is happening in this
scene. What do the hearts on Jesus' shoulders symbolize?

_____

_____

_____

_____

_____

_____

He was pierced for our rebellion, crushed for our sins. He was beaten
so we could be whole. He was whipped so we could be healed.
All of us, like sheep, have strayed away.
We have left God's paths to follow our own.
Yet the LORD laid on him the sins of us all.
Isaiah 53:5-6 NLT

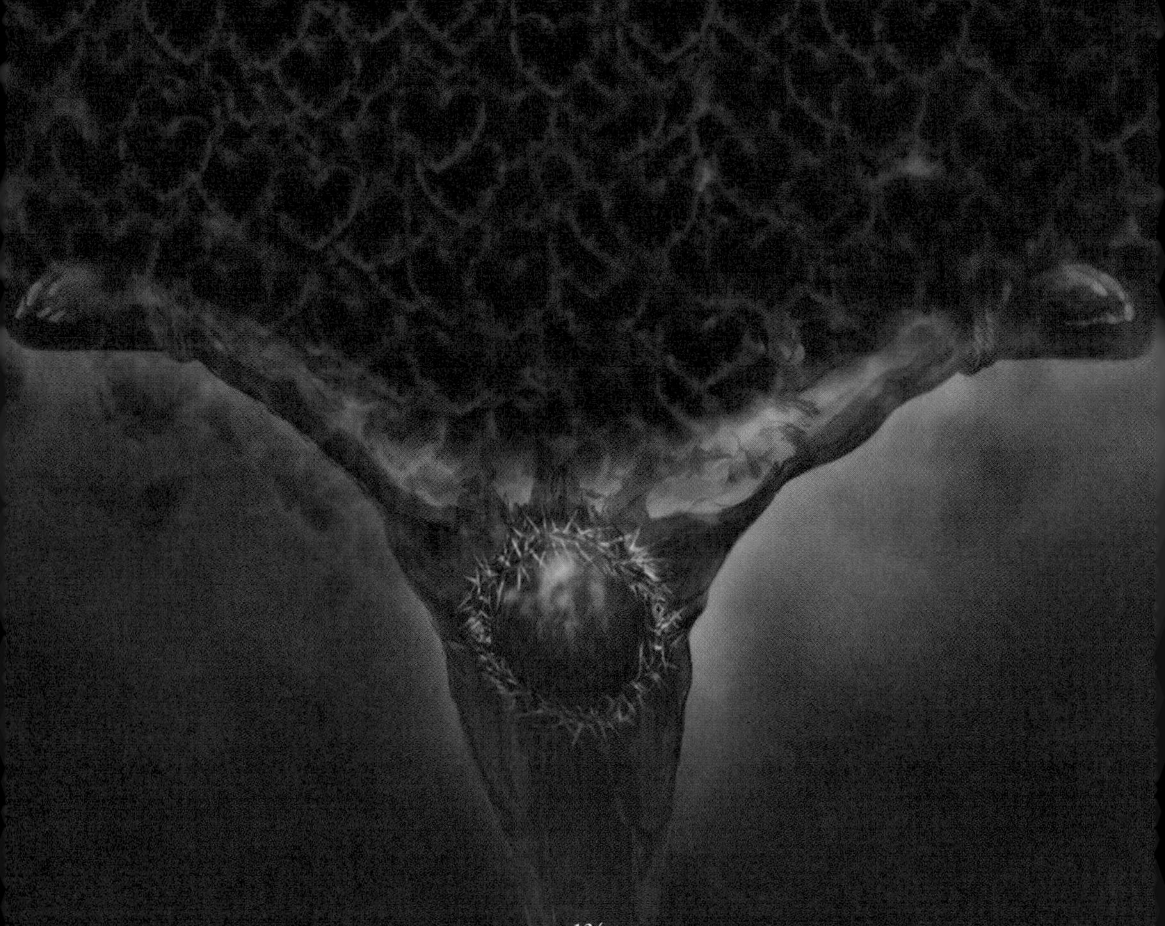

B Answer the following questions.

1. What did *not* happen after Jesus had been on the cross for three hours?

   a. It became dark. b. The onlookers scattered.

   c. It became silent. d. God in heaven comforted Jesus.

2. What did Jesus say on the cross? "My God, my God, why have you
   _____ me?" (Matthew 27:46).

   a. crucified b. forsaken

3. Jesus' cross was like an altar in the Old Testament,
   and Jesus was like _____.

   a. a knife b. a lamb

4. What did God put on His holy Son on the cross?

   a. our sins, as a sin offering

   b. nothing, He died as a martyr

5. After Jesus had absorbed the punishment sinners deserve and
   fulfilled the prophecies of the Old Testament, what did He say
   just before He died?

   a. "The end is near." b. "It is finished!"

6. What did *not* happen right after Jesus died?

   a. The earth shook. b. The curtain in the temple was torn.

   c. The rocks split. d. God killed the men who killed His Son.

7. When Jesus died, God tore open the curtain that hid the special room
   in the temple where animal blood was sprinkled each year to cover sin.
   Why is animal blood no longer required to cover sin?

   _____

   _____

   _____

   _____

14

64 THE KING IS BURIED

📖 MATTHEW 27

A Answer the following questions.

1. How did the soldiers confirm that Jesus was dead?

    a. They jabbed a spear into His side.

    b. They asked a medical examiner.

2. Jesus' disciples had been expecting Him to crush the Romans and set up an earthly kingdom. Complete the following sentence to explain how you think they felt when they realized He was dead.

    When the disciples realized that Jesus was dead, they felt...

3. The dead bodies of crucified victims were usually tossed onto a garbage dump outside the city or into a mass grave. How was Jesus' burial different? Explain what happened to Jesus' body after He died.

B Mark the following statements true or false.

1. The religious leaders knew Jesus had promised that after three days He would come back to life.　　True　False

2. The religious leaders asked Pilate to make the tomb secure so Jesus' body could not be stolen.　　True　False

3. Pilate gave the religious leaders permission to secure the tomb.　　True　False

4. The religious leaders themselves guarded the tomb.　　True　False

He was assigned a grave with the wicked,
　and with the rich in his death....
　　—PROPHET ISAIAH (ISAIAH 53:9)

136

65 THE EMPTY TOMB

📖 MATTHEW 28

A Number the pictures so they match the order of events.

1. The soldiers were guarding the tomb where Jesus was buried.
2. Several women came to the tomb early Sunday morning.
3. Suddenly, there was a great earthquake as an angel came down from heaven, pushed aside the stone, and sat on it. The soldiers fainted.
4. The angel told the women, "[Jesus] isn't here! He has been raised from the dead, just as he said would happen."
5. Jesus met the women as they ran from the tomb to tell the disciples.
6. The religious leaders bribed the soldiers to lie and tell others that Jesus' disciples came during the night and stole his body.

"Don't be afraid! I am the First and the Last.
    I am the living one who died.
       Look, I am alive forever and ever!
And I hold the keys of death and the grave."

—THE RISEN KING (REVELATION 1:17-18 NLT)

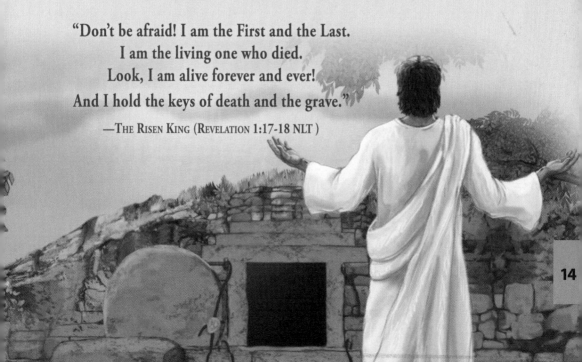

B   Fill in the blanks with the words from the box below.

By His _____,
Jesus paid our sin debt.

By His _____,
Jesus went down into
the pit of death.

By His _____.
Jesus overcame death.

burial • resurrection • death

It is this Good News that saves you if you firmly believe it …
Christ died for our sins, just as the Scriptures said. He was buried,
and he was raised from the dead on the third day, as the Scriptures said.
1 CORINTHIANS 15:2-4 NLT

An inside view of the Garden Tomb.[5]
The angel said to the women, "Don't be afraid! I know you are looking for Jesus,
who was crucified. He isn't here! He has been raised from the dead,
just as he said would happen. Come, see where his body was lying" (Matthew 28:5-6).

C Look at the timeline and choose the right word order.

In Old Testament times, those who trusted God and His plan looked
_____ to what God would do to save them from their sins.
Today, in New Testament times, we who trust God and His plan, look
_____ at what God has done to save us from our sins.

a. back, forward   b. forward, back

Old Testament   New Testament

The Garden Tomb.
This could be the tomb in which Jesus was buried. Just a few minutes walk from *The Place of the Skull*, it fits with what Scripture says. *"At the place where Jesus was crucified, there was a garden, and in the garden a new tomb, in which no one had ever been laid"* (John 19:41).

EPISODE 15
THE KING'S GOSPEL & GLORY

KING of GLORY • SCENES 66–70

INTRODUCE

What does the Messiah's death, burial, and resurrection mean to you?

After suffering the punishment our sins require, Jesus died. His corpse was removed from the cross and laid in a tomb. But three days later, He came back to life in a glorious body never to die again!

Death is a great enemy. Our ancestors died. The prophets also died, and their corpses returned to dust. But Jesus defeated death. By paying for our sins and rising from the dead, He is the first to conquer death, but He will not be the last! If I put my trust in Him and what He did for me, I need not fear death, for it is merely the door into the actual presence of my King *"who loved me and gave himself for me!"* (Galatians 2:20). The same is true for you and all who, from the heart, believe in Him.

The resurrection of Jesus the Messiah is the greatest event in human history, which is why the Scriptures declare, *"[God] now commands all people everywhere to repent. For He has set a day when He will judge the world with justice by the Man He has appointed. He has given proof of this to all men by raising Him from the dead"* (Acts 17:30-31).

Do you believe that the King of glory died for you and defeated death for you? Is He your Savior? Or will He be your Judge?

It is time for the final stage of our journey.

WATCH (🕐18:26)

Episode 15 covers **Scenes 66–70**

DISCUSS

1. What surprised you in this episode?

2. On the day of Jesus' resurrection, why were the two travelers on the road to Emmaus so sad? Why did Jesus call them "foolish"?

3. Name some Old Testament prophecies (such as Psalm 22:16-18) or pictures (such as Genesis 22:1-14) that Jesus the Messiah fulfilled.

4. Thomas said to the risen Lord, *"My Lord and My God!"* Was Thomas right or wrong to call Jesus his "Lord" and his "God"?

5. Why was it necessary for Jesus the Messiah to die on the cross and rise from the dead?

6. How can you go from being "in Adam" to being "in Christ"?

7. Tell about Jesus' last forty days on earth before He returned to Heaven. What did He do? What did He say?

8. After Jesus returns to earth, what will happen to Satan and his kingdom of darkness? What will happen to the citizens of the kingdom of light?

9. How has God's story and message touched your mind and heart?

10. Who is this King of glory? What has He done *for you*? Do you love Him?

REFLECT

For as in Adam all die, so in Christ all will be made alive. (1 Corinthians 15:22)

All the prophets testify about [the risen Lord Jesus] that everyone who believes in him receives forgiveness of sins through his name. (Acts 10:43)

REINFORCE

Review Episode 15
by doing the activities
on the next pages.

66 THE MESSAGE OF THE PROPHETS

📖 LUKE 24

A Answer the following questions.

1. What were the two disciples discussing intently on the road to Emmaus?

    a. The political tensions in the Roman empire.

    b. The events that had just taken place in Jerusalem.

    c. The many ancient prophecies that foretold the sufferings, crucifixion, burial, and resurrection of the Messiah.

2. Why did they not recognize Jesus when He joined them?

    a. Jesus was dressed in unfamiliar clothing.

    b. They were too busy talking to each other.

    c. God kept them from recognizing Him.

3. What confused the disciples the most about Jesus of Nazareth?

    a. Jesus' miracles.   b. Jesus' crucifixion.

    c. Jesus' resurrection.   d. Jesus' power over His enemies.

4. What did Jesus do to help the disciples understand what had happened to the Messiah? Jesus showed them that (Choose two answers.)

    a. the prophets had clearly predicted the Messiah's suffering.

    b. His next move would be to conquer Rome.

    c. the Scriptures of Moses and the prophets all point to Him.

B How has understanding the message of the prophets helped you understand who Jesus is and what He came to accomplish?

_____

_____

_____

_____

Then Jesus took them through the writings of Moses and all the prophets, explaining from all the Scriptures the things concerning himself.

LUKE 24:27 NLT

C If we understand how Jesus fulfilled the Old Testament prophecies, the message of the prophets makes perfect sense. Fill in the blanks with the words from the boxes at the bottom of each page.

1. The prophets predicted that the **Messiah** would be _____ in Bethlehem (Micah 5:1-2), born of a virgin (Isaiah 7:14), and born of the family line of _____ (Jeremiah 23:5). They also said that Jesus would be announced by a forerunner (the prophet John) who would _____ the way for Him (Isaiah 40:3). Jesus fulfilled these prophecies.

2. Isaiah predicted that the _____ would perform miracles such as _____ the blind, deaf, lame, and mute (Isaiah 35:4-6). Jesus performed all these miracles.

healing • born • David • Messiah • prepare • Messiah

3. The prophet Zechariah had predicted the Messiah's entry into
    _____ riding on a _____ (Zechariah 9:9).

4. The prophets had predicted that the Messiah would be _____
    and gloated over. David predicted that they would divide His
    _____ among them and cast lots for them, that they would
    mock and _____ Him (Psalm 22:6-8, 16-18; Isaiah 53:5-6). These
    very things happened to _____.

    insult • Jesus • pierced • donkey • Jerusalem • garments

5. The prophets predicted that the _____ would take the _____ for our sins. They said He would be pierced, crushed, beaten, and whipped—just as Jesus was—so that we would not have to receive the punishment for our sins and so that we could be _____ (Isaiah 53:5-6). The prophet Abraham predicted that God would provide a _____ for the burnt offering (Genesis 22:8). The prophet John called Jesus the "Lamb of God" (John 1:29, 36).

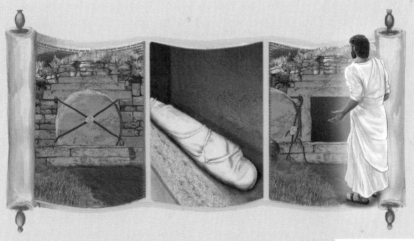

6. Isaiah predicted that the Messiah would be "assigned a _____ with the wicked, and with the rich in his death " (Isaiah 53:9). David foretold that God would not allow His Holy One to undergo _____ (Psalm 16:10). These prophecies foretold Jesus' burial and resurrection.

> grave • punishment • Messiah • decay • healed • Lamb

67 A TRANSFORMED BODY

📖 JOHN 20, 1 CORINTHIANS 15

A Answer the following questions.

1. Which one did Thomas *not* say he needed to do?

   a. Put his finger in the nail marks in Jesus' hands.

   b. Touch Jesus' forehead, where the crown of thorns had been.

   c. Put his hand into Jesus' side, which had been pierced.

2. What did Jesus tell Thomas when he appeared to him?

   a. "Stop doubting and believe."

   b. "Great is your faith!"

3. What did Thomas call Jesus?

   a. "My King!"   b. "My prophet!""

   c. "My Master and my Teacher."   d. "My Lord and my God!"

4. Jesus told Thomas, "Because you have _____ me, you have believed; blessed are those who have not _____ and yet have believed."

   a. seen, seen   b. touched, touched

5. After His resurrection, how many more days did Jesus spend on earth?

   a. 40   b. 100

6. How was Jesus' body different than yours and mine? Who else will someday receive a transformed body similar to His?

_____

_____

_____

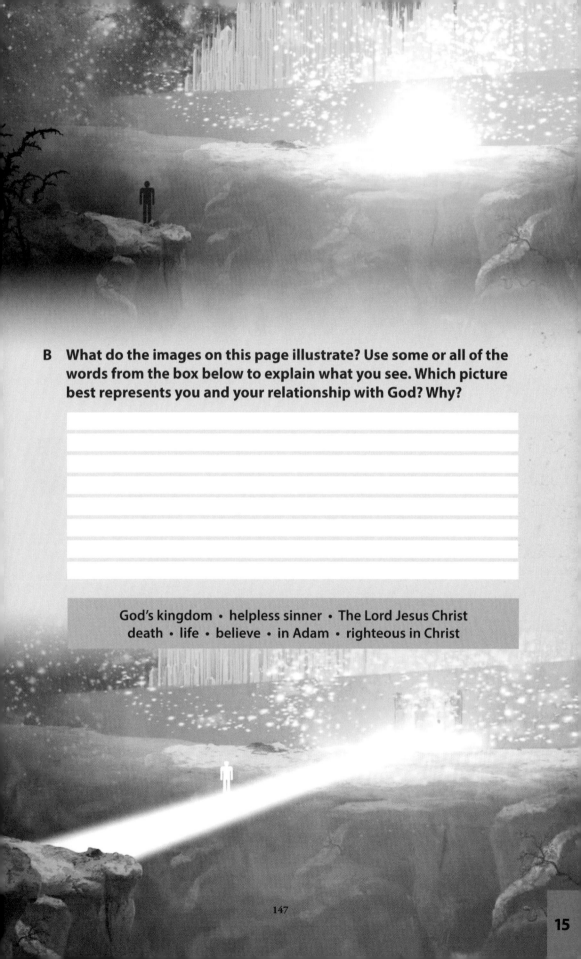

B What do the images on this page illustrate? Use some or all of the words from the box below to explain what you see. Which picture best represents you and your relationship with God? Why?

God's kingdom · helpless sinner · The Lord Jesus Christ
death · life · believe · in Adam · righteous in Christ

68 THE DEPARTURE

📖 ACTS 1

A   Mark the following statements true or false.

1. Jesus was unable to stop the religious leaders and   True   False
    soldiers from arresting, torturing, and crucifying Him.

2. Jesus gathered His disciples on Mount Sinai before   True   False
    He returned to His Father's home.

3. Jesus promised to always be with His disciples,   True   False
    even though He was leaving the earth.

4. Jesus' message was to be taught to all nations.   True   False

5. Jesus gave the disciples a date for His return.   True   False

6. Jesus disappeared into the sky.   True   False

> "All authority in heaven and on earth has been given to me.
> Therefore go and make disciples of all nations...." MATTHEW 28:18-19

B   Answer the following questions.

1. Give some examples of how Jesus showed His authority over
    the devil and demons, wind and waves, sickness and hunger,
    sin and death.

    _____

    _____

    _____

    _____

2. What assignments did Jesus give His
    disciples before leaving? (Matthew 28:18-20)

    _____

    _____

3. How should people be able to identify
    Jesus' disciples? (John 13:34-35)

    _____

    _____

69 THE VICTORY CELEBRATION

📖 PSALM 24; REVELATION 5

A   Answer the following questions.

1. Imagine the scene when Jesus returned to Heaven after He accomplished His mission on earth. He is received as a King who has won a battle. What is the battle that Jesus won? How did He win it?

2. What difference does it make to you to know that Jesus won the battle?

3. Who can live in the celestial city with Jesus? How do you know this?

B   Connect the beginning of each verse on the left with the correct ending of the verse on the right.

1. "Who is the King of glory? …

2. "Worthy is the Lamb, who was slain, to receive …

3. "I am the way, the truth, and the life …

4. "Don't let your hearts be troubled, …

5. When everything is ready, I will come and get you …

6. "You are worthy … for you were killed, and your blood has …

a. no one can come to the Father except through me" (John 14:6 NLT).

b. ransomed people for God from every tribe and language and people and nation" (Rev. 5:9 NLT).

c. so that you will always be with me where I am" (John 14:3 NLT).

d. trust in God, and trust also in me. There is more than enough room in my Father's home" (John 14:1-2 NLT).

e. the LORD Almighty—he is the King of glory!" (Psalm 24:10 NLT).

f. honor and glory and praise!" (Revelation 5:12).

149

15

70 THE KING IS COMING BACK

📖 REVELATION 19-22

A **The Scriptures speak of several things that will happen when the King comes back. Connect the words with the related pictures.**

1. The King of glory will return to Earth on a white horse. He will reign, make war against His enemies, and show the world what a righteous government looks like.

a.

2. On the Day of Judgment, the LORD Jesus will be the Judge of all who rejected Him as their Savior.

b.

3. King Jesus will bind Satan and eventually throw both Satan and all his followers into the Lake of Fire.

c.

4. God will make a new heaven and a new earth.

d.

5. God will wipe every tear from the eyes of the citizens of the kingdom of light. There will be no more death or mourning or crying.

e.

B **Are you a citizen of the kingdom of light, or of the kingdom of darkness? How do you know? Is the King of glory *your* king?**

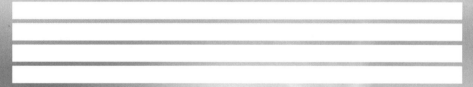

Good News

The Scriptures tell many stories of what God's Holy Spirit did in the lives of people after Jesus returned to heaven. For example, in the book of Acts, chapter 16, we read the story of a cruel jail guard in Philippi who asked two of Jesus' disciples: *"Sirs, what must I do to be saved?"* (Acts 16:30).

A   In brief, based on what you know from the Scriptures, how would you answer the jailer's question?

Here is how the two disciples answered the jailer: "Believe in the Lord Jesus, and you will be saved—you and your household!" (Acts 16:31).

You can read the full story in Acts, chapter 16. It tells about the disciples going to the jailer's home and telling him and his family about Jesus, the Savior foretold by the prophets. That night, the father, mother, children, and all who lived with them, understood and believed God's way of salvation. Because of their faith in the Lord Jesus and what He did for them on the cross, their sins were forgiven, they were made right in God's eyes, and the Holy Spirit came to live in their hearts. Their lives were changed! And to show that they had become citizens of God's kingdom, they were baptized in water, symbolizing their oneness with the Lord Jesus Christ in His death, burial, and resurrection.

B   In your own words, tell and explain God's good news for sinners.

Note: If you want to write it out instead of just telling it, use a separate piece of paper.

*It is this Good News that saves you ... **Christ died for our sins,** just as the Scriptures said. **He was buried,** and he was **raised from the dead** on the third day, just as the Scriptures said* (1 Corinthians 15:2-4 NLT).

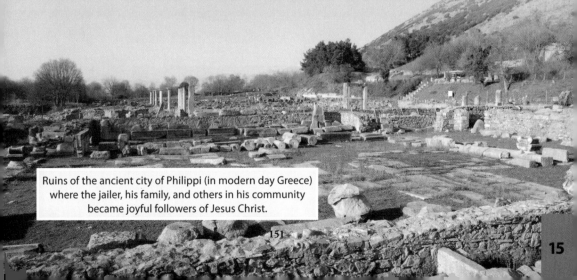

Ruins of the ancient city of Philippi (in modern day Greece) where the jailer, his family, and others in his community became joyful followers of Jesus Christ.

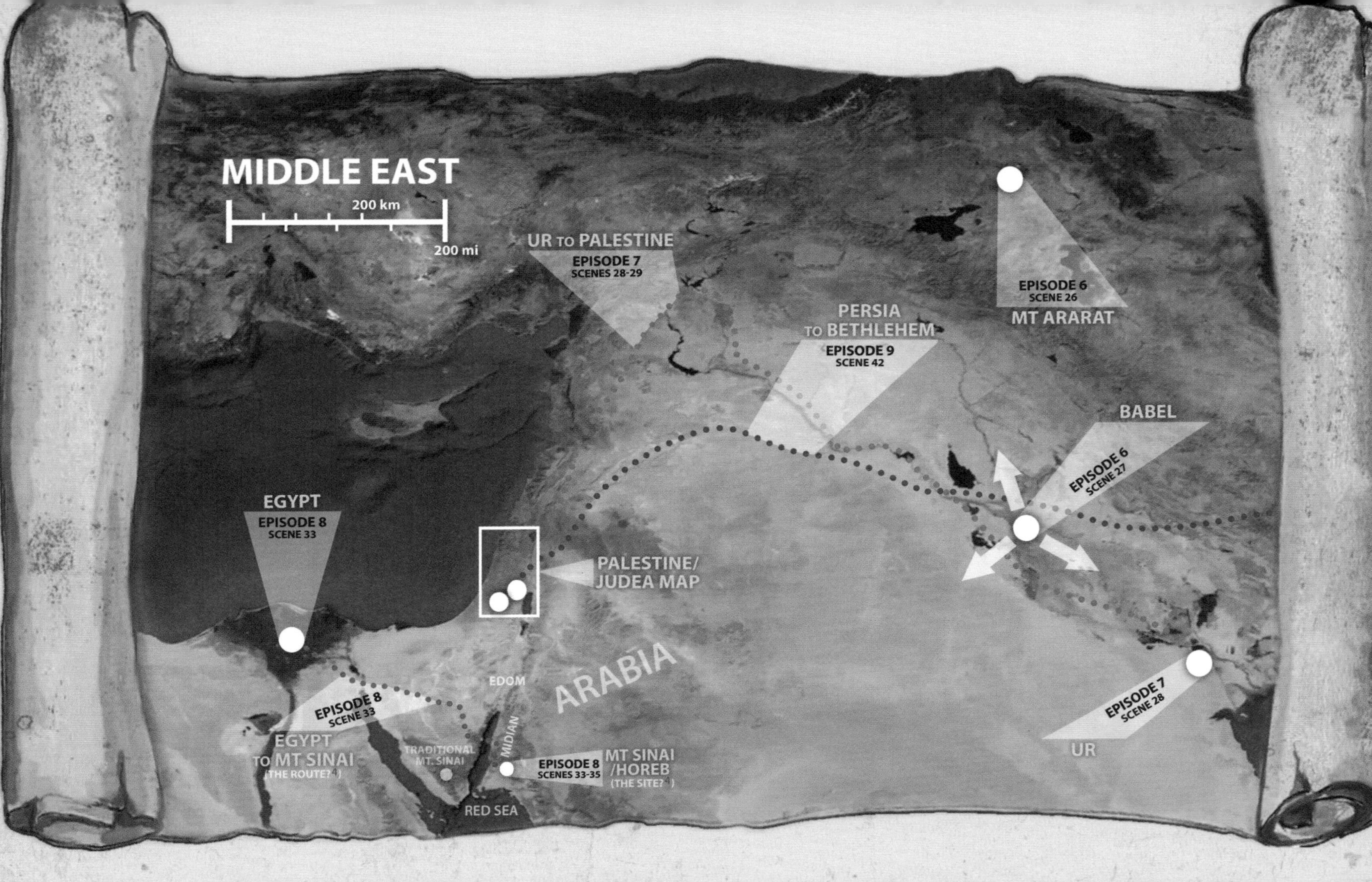

MIDDLE EAST

200 km

200 mi

EGYPT
EPISODE 8
SCENE 33

EGYPT
TO MT SINAI
(THE ROUTE)
EPISODE 8
SCENE 33

TRADITIONAL
MT SINAI

RED SEA

MIDIAN

EDOM

MT SINAI
/HOREB
(THE SITE?)
EPISODE 8
SCENES 33-35

ARABIA

PALESTINE/
JUDEA MAP

UR TO PALESTINE
EPISODE 7
SCENES 28-29

PERSIA
TO BETHLEHEM
EPISODE 9
SCENE 42

MT ARARAT
EPISODE 6
SCENE 26

EPISODE 6
SCENE 27

BABEL

UR

EPISODE 7
SCENE 28

PALESTINE/
JUDEA

20 km

0   20 mi

NAZARETH

EPISODE 9, 19
SCENES 38, 39, 47

EPISODE 11
SCENES 48, 50

CAPERNAUM

EPISODES 11, 12
SCENES 48-49, 52-53

WEST SIDE OF GALILEE

EPISODE 11
SCENE 51

EPISODE 12
SCENE 54

NAIN   MT TABOR

EPISODE 10
SCENE 43

BETHLEHEM
TO EGYPT
TO NAZARETH

EPISODE 9
SCENE 40

NAZARETH
TO
BETHLEHEM

JORDAN RIVER

EPISODE 10
SCENES 44, 45

MT MORIAH

EPISODE 14
SCENES 61-65

JERUSALEM

EPISODE 13, 15
SCENES 56-60, 67-68

EPISODE 9
SCENE 42

EMMAUS

EPISODE 15
SCENE 66

PERSIA
TO JERUSALEM
TO BETHLEHEM

BETHLEHEM

EPISODE 9
SCENE 41

EPISODE 11
SCENE 51

HEBRON
(ABRAHAM'S HOME)

EPISODE 7
SCENE 30

BETHANY

DESERT

EPISODE 10
SCENE 46

KING OF GLORY MOVIE
EPISODE & SCENE LENGTHS

PART 1 THE KING FORETELLS HIS PLAN (OLD TESTAMENT)

EPISODE #	TITLE	SCENE #	START TIME	DURATION
1	**Prologue**	**1-3**		**10:40**
	The King and His Kingdom	1	0:00	4:40
	The King and His Prophets	2	4:40	2:59
	The King and His Universe	3	7:39	3:01
2	**The Creator & His Creation**	**4-9**		**19:04**
	The First Day	4	10:40	3:39
	A Perfect World	5	14:19	3:38
	The First Man	6	17:57	3:12
	A Perfect Home	7	21:09	3:03
	The Law of Sin and Death	8	24:12	2:53
	The First Woman	9	27:05	2:40
3	**Evil's Entrance**	**10-15**		**15:10**
	The Kingdom of Light	10	29:45	3:11
	The Kingdom of Darkness	11	32:56	3:10
	The Serpent	12	36:06	2:35
	The Choice	13	38:41	1:43
	Sin and Shame	14	40:24	2:06
	Spiritually Dead	15	42:30	2:24
4	**Sin's Curse & God's Promise**	**16-19**		**11:57**
	The Curse	16	44:54	3:24
	The Promise	17	48:18	2:48
	The First Sacrifice	18	51:06	2:39
	Banished	19	53:45	3:07
5	**The Way of the Sacrifice**	**20-24**		**14:58**
	The First Children	20	56:52	3:16
	Sinners Worship	21	1:00:08	2:31
	The Law of the Sin Offering	22	1:02:39	3:09
	Accepted and Rejected	23	1:05:48	3:07
	The First Murder	24	1:08:55	2:55
6	**Man's Rebellion & God's Faithfulness**	**25-27**		**9:05**
	Patience and Judgment	25	1:11:50	3:45
	A Fresh Start	26	1:15:35	2:45
	The Tower of Pride	27	1:18:20	2:35
7	**God's Plan Advances**	**28-32**		**14:04**
	God Calls Abraham	28	1:20:55	3:07
	The Promise Keeper	29	1:24:02	3:06
	The Ultimate Test	30	1:27:08	2:50
	The Condemned Son	31	1:29:58	2:28
	Pictures and Prophecies	32	1:32:26	2:33
8	**The Law & The Prophets**	**33-36**		**12:20**
	A Faithful and Holy God	33	1:34:59	3:43
	The Ten Commandments	34	1:38:42	4:12
	More Pictures	35	1:42:54	2:48
	More Prophecies	36	1:45:42	1:33

PART 1 RUN TIME: **1 hour 47 minutes**

This chart provides a list with the title, start time, and length of each episode and each scene. The *KING OF GLORY* book has 70 scenes (or chapters). The *KING OF GLORY* movie groups those 70 scenes into 15 episodes. In the movie, each time you see the book on the table, it is the beginning of a new episode. Every time you see a page turn, it is the start of a new scene.

PART 2 THE KING FULFILLS HIS PLAN (NEW TESTAMENT)

EPISODE #	TITLE	SCENE #	START TIME	DURATION
9	**The King's Entrance**	**37-42**		**20:16**
	The King's Story Continues	37	0:00	4:03
	Mary's Story	38	4:03	3:43
	Joseph's Story	39	7:46	2:57
	The Arrival	40	10:43	2:59
	The Shepherds' Story	41	13:42	3:05
	The Magi's Story	42	16:47	3:28
10	**The King's Character**	**43-47**		**15:32**
	The Perfect Child	43	20:15	3:04
	The Lamb of God	44	23:19	3:02
	The Perfect Son	45	26:21	3:17
	The Second Man	46	29:38	3:43
	The Messiah-King	47	33:21	2:25
11	**The King's Dominion**	**48-51**		**14:02**
	Dominion over Demons and Disease	48	35:46	3:23
	Dominion over Wind and Waves	49	39:09	3:16
	Dominion over Sin	50	42:25	3:13
	Dominion over Death	51	45:38	4:12
12	**The King's Mission**	**52-56**		**15:24**
	The Provider	52	49:50	3:10
	The Teacher	53	53:00	3:20
	His Majesty	54	56:20	3:11
	His Mission	55	59:31	2:50
	The King Enters Jerusalem	56	1:02:21	2:52
13	**The King's Submission**	**57-61**		**14:50**
	The King is Questioned	57	1:05:13	3:08
	The King is Arrested	58	1:08:21	3:12
	The King is Condemned	59	1:11:33	2:40
	The King is Crowned	60	1:14:13	2:36
	The King is Crucified	61	1:16:49	3:15
14	**The King's Sacrifice & Triumph**	**62-65**		**13:53**
	The Savior-King	62	1:20:04	3:33
	The Final Sacrifice	63	1:23:37	3:59
	The King is Buried	64	1:27:36	3:05
	The Empty Tomb	65	1:30:41	3:16
15	**The King's Gospel & Glory**	**66-70**		**18:26**
	The Message of the Prophets	66	1:33:57	3:40
	A Transformed Body	67	1:37:37	2:55
	The Departure	68	1:40:32	3:04
	Victory Celebration	69	1:43:36	3:47
	The King is Coming Back	70	1:47:23	5:05
Credits	*How Great is Our God (Sung in Arabic)*		1:52:28	2:30

PART 2 RUN TIME: 1 hour 55 minutes

TOTAL RUN TIME: 3 hours 42 minutes

KING OF GLORY
RELATED SCRIPTURES

PART 1 THE KING FORETELLS HIS PLAN (OLD TESTAMENT)

SCENE #	MAIN SCRIPTURE	EXTRA SCRIPTURES
Episode 1 • Prologue		
1	—	Psalm 24; Psalm 103:19-22; 1 Timothy 1:17
2	—	Psalm 119; 2 Peter 1:16-21; 2 Timothy 3:14-17; 2:15
3	—	Psalm 19; Romans 1:18-25; Hebrews 11:3; Acts 17:24-28
Episode 2 • The Creator & His Creation		
4	Genesis 1	Nehemiah 9:6; Job 26:7; Psalm 33:6-9; 90:2; 102:25; Deuteronomy 6:4; Exodus 3:13-15; Isaiah 6:3; 1 John 1:5; John 1:1-5; Revelation 4:8
5	Genesis 1-2	1 John 1:5-6; Psalm 33:9; Timothy 6:17b; Psalm 89:37; John 1:3-4; 1 John 4:8
6	Genesis 1-2	Psalm 8; 1 Corinthians 15:39; 1 Thessalonians 5:23; Hebrews 4:12; John 15:14-15; Galatians 4:7
7	Genesis 2	Psalm 115:16; Isaiah 42:5; 45:18; Luke 16:10; Romans 5:19
8	Genesis 2	Isaiah 59:2; Ezekiel 18:4b; James 1:15; Romans 5:12; 6:23; 8:2
9	Genesis 2	Galatians 3:26-28; Ephesians 5:22-33; 2 Corinthians 11:2-3; Revelation 19:7-8; 21:2
Episode 3 • Evil's Entrance		
10	Revelation 4-5	Job 19:25-27; 1 Corinthians 2:7-10; Revelation 4:1-3; 7:9-10; 21:1-27; 22:1-5
11	Isaiah 14:12-17; Ezekiel 28:11-17	2 Corinthians 4:3-4; 11:14; Ephesians 2:2; 1 Peter 5:8-9
12	Genesis 3	Walking with God: Genesis 3:8a; 5:22-24; 6:9; Leviticus 26:12; Micah 6:8; Deceived by Satan: 2 Corinthians 11:3; Revelation 12:9; John 8:44
13	Genesis 3	1 Timothy 2:13-14; Romans 5:12; James 1:15; 1 John 2:16; Hebrews 9:27
14	Genesis 3	Genesis 2:25; 3:7-8; Isaiah 43:27
15	Genesis 3	Isaiah 59:2; Romans 5:12-21; 1 Corinthians 5:21-22
Episode 4 • Sin's Curse & God's Promise		
16	Genesis 3	Romans 5:12-14; 8:2; Ezekiel 18:20; Hebrews 9:27; Revelation 20:11-15; 21:27
17	Genesis 3	Isaiah 7:14; 9:2; Galatians 4:4; 1 Corinthians 15:45-47; Micah 5:2
18	Genesis 3	Deuteronomy 32:4; Isaiah 30:18; 61:10; Romans 3:19-26; Ephesians 2:1-10; Titus 3:4-7; Revelation 7:9-14; 22:14;
19	Genesis 3	Psalm 89:14, 34-35; Numbers 23:19; Hebrews 9:27
Episode 5 • The Way of the Sacrifice		
20	Genesis 4	Genesis 3:16-24; Psalm 51:5; 58:3; Romans 5:12; 8:20-22; 1 Corinthians 15:22a
21	Genesis 4	Romans 8:2; Hebrews 9:22, 27
22	Genesis 4	Leviticus 17:11; 1:4; 6:25; Deuteronomy 14:7-8; Hebrews 9:22
23	Genesis 4	Leviticus 17:11; Hebrews 9:22 and 11:4
24	Genesis 4-5	1 John 3:11-12; Mark 1:15; Acts 20:21; 26:20; 1 Thessalonians 1:9; Galatians 6:8
Episode 6 • Man's Rebellion & God's Faithfulness		
25	Genesis 6-7	Nahum 1:3a; Exodus 34:5-7; 1 Peter 3:20; 2 Peter 2:5; 3:3-9
26	Genesis 8-9	Hebrews 10:7; 9:22; Leviticus 17:11
27	Genesis 11	Ezekiel 28:17; Jeremiah 9:23-24; James 4:6-10; Ephesians 2:8-10; 1 Corinthians 1:31
Episode 7 • God's Plan Advances		
28	Genesis 12	Genesis 12:2-3; 17:1-8; 18:18; 22:17-18; Galatians 3:7-9; Hebrews 11:8-10
29	Genesis 15-17, 21	Genesis 15:6; Romans 4:1-5; James 2:23; Hebrews 11:11-16
30	Genesis 22	Hebrews 11:17; James 2:18-26; John 1:29
31	Genesis 22	Hebrews 11:17-19
32	Genesis 22	John 8:56-58; 3:16; 1:29; 19:30; 1 Peter 1:17-21
Episode 8 • The Law & The Prophets		
33	Exodus 19-20	Job 9:2, 30-33; Psalm 51:5-10; Proverbs 20:9; Isaiah 64:6
34	Exodus 20	Deuteronomy 27:26; Romans 3:10-12,19-20; James 1:23; 2:10
35	Exodus 20, 24	Leviticus 1:4; 17:11; Hebrews 9:22; 10:1-23
36	Psalms & Prophets	Psalm 2:6-12; 22:1-22; 16:9-10; Isaiah 7:14; 9:6; 35:4-6; 52:13-53:12, etc.

This chart is a supplementary resource for teachers and students who want to dig deeper into the Word of God. These references are not meant to be read in conjunction with the study, as that would take too much time and could even confuse some students, since many of these verses, while supporting the teaching in the scene, relate to a different time and context.

Do your best to present yourself to God as one approved, a worker who does not need to be ashamed and who correctly handles the word of truth (2 Timothy 2:15).

PART 2 THE KING FULFILLS HIS PLAN (NEW TESTAMENT)

SCENE #	MAIN SCRIPTURE	EXTRA SCRIPTURES
Episode 9 • The King's Entrance		
37	**Matthew 1**	Jeremiah 31:31-34; Hebrews 8:6-13; Luke 1:1-4; John 20:30-31; 2 Peter 3:15-16
38	**Luke 1**	Genesis 3:15; Galatians 4:4; Matthew 1:23; John 1:1-3,14
39	**Matthew 1**	Luke 1:26-27; Isaiah 7:14; 9:2, 6-7
40	**Luke 2**	Genesis 3:15; Micah 5:2; Isaiah 7:14; John 1:1-5;14; 3:16
41	**Luke 2**	Isaiah 6:1-3; 9:2; 60:1-3; 1 Timothy 3:16
42	**Matthew 2**	Psalm 2; Micah 5:2; John 18:37; 1 Timothy 1:15; 1 Corinthians 15:1-4
Episode 10 • The King's Character		
43	**Luke 2**	Luke 2:40, 52; Mark 6:3; Hebrews 2:14-18; 4:15; 7:26; 1 Peter 2:22
44	**Matthew 3, John 1**	Isaiah 40:3-5; Malachi 3:1; John 1:29; Genesis 3:21; 22:8-15; Hebrews 7:27; 10:1-18
45	**Matthew 3**	Genesis 1:1-3; Isaiah 48:16; John 1:1-3; 10:30; Matthew 28:18-20; Hebrews 1:1-3; 7:26-27
46	**Matthew 4**	Luke 4:1-13; Hebrews 4:14-16; Romans 5:12-19; 1 Corinthians 15:21-22, 45-47
47	**Luke 4**	Luke 4:14-31; Isaiah 61:1-2; John 8:59; 10:39; 18:6-7
Episode 11 • The King's Dominion		
48	**Luke 4**	Isaiah 35:4-6; 61:1; Matthew 4:15-25; 15:30-31; Mark 1:15
49	**Mark 4**	Psalm 33:6-7; 89:8-9; 107:27-29; Matthew 8:23-27; 14:22-33
50	**Mark 2**	Psalm 32:1-5; Matthew 9:2; Isaiah 43:11; Acts 4:12; 10:43; Romans 3:19-26
51	**Luke 7; John 11**	Job 19:25-27; Mark 5:21-43; John 5:22-29; Revelation 1:17-18
Episode 12 • The King's Mission		
52	**John 6**	John 6:35, 48; Matthew 11:28-30; Luke 12:16-21; 16:19-31; 2 Corinthians 4:16-18
53	**Matthew 5-7**	John 13:34-35; 14:1-6; Matthew 24:24-25; Luke 6:46-49
54	**Matthew 17**	Isaiah 9:2; Malachi 4:2; John 1:4-5,14; 3:19-20; 8:12; 9:5; 2 Peter 1:16-18
55	**Mathew 16, 20**	Matthew 16:21-23; 20:17-19; Mark 8:30-32; Luke 9:21-22; 18:31-34; John 13:19
56	**Mark 11**	Zechariah 9:9; Matthew 21:1-11; John 12:9-19
Episode 13 • The King's Submission		
57	**Luke 20**	Matthew 22:15-46; Colossians 2:2-4
58	**Mark 14**	Matthew 26:1-4; 51-56; John 18:1-14; Luke 22:47-71
59	**John 18**	Matthew 27:1-26
60	**Matthew 27**	Matthew 27: 26-32
61	**Luke 23**	Matthew 27:33-43; Genesis 22:7-14; Psalm 22:1-18; Isaiah 53:4-7
Episode 14 • The King's Sacrifice & Triumph		
62	**Luke 23**	Genesis 3:15; 1 Corinthians 2:7-8; Isaiah 53:11-12; John 3:14-18
63	**Matthew 27**	John 19:30; Isaiah 53:4-6; 2 Corinthians 5:17-21; 1 Peter 2:22-25; 3:18
64	**Matthew 27**	Isaiah 53:9; Mark 15:40-47; John 19:38-42;
65	**Matthew 28**	Psalm 16:10; Mark 16:1-8; John 20:1-18; Luke 24:1-12; 1 Corinthians 15:1-8
Episode 15 • The King's Gospel & Glory		
66	**Luke 24**	Genesis 3:15, 21; 22:8-15; Psalm 22; Isaiah 53; Luke 24:25-27; Acts 10:43; 26:22-23, 27
67	**John 20**	1 Corinthians 15:35-57; Philippians 3:20-21; 1 John 3:1-3
68	**Acts 1**	Matthew 28:18-20; Luke 24:36-53
69	**Psalm 24; Revelation 5**	John 3:13; 1 Peter 3:22; Hebrews 1:3; Psalm 110:1; John 14:1-6; 1 Timothy 3:16
70	**Revelation 19-22**	Genesis 3:15; Daniel 7:9-10; Colossians 1:12-14; 2 Timothy 1:9-10; Romans 10:9

The Message in the Story

"I tell you the truth, whoever hears my word and believes him who sent me has eternal life and will not be condemned; he has crossed over from death to life!"

— JESUS, KING OF GLORY (GOSPEL OF JOHN 5:24)

The following summary of God's way of salvation is from the *KING OF GLORY* book.

In English, this summary is also available as a Special Feature at **www.king-of-glory.com** and on the *KING OF GLORY* DVD, Edition 2.

HAPPILY EVER AFTER?

People of all ages love imaginary tales of romance and rescue, stories with happy endings. People tell such tales because the one true God has built into the human heart a yearning to be delivered from evil and to live happily ever after. But the story of the King of glory is no imaginary tale.

 A make-believe story is not written by forty prophets over fifteen centuries, but God's book is. Fiction is not confirmed by hundreds of prophecies and archaeological discoveries, but God's story is.

 A make-believe superhero is not the dividing point of history, but Jesus is. Fantasy cannot remove our sin and shame, bring us to God, and give us a new heart filled with His love, joy, and peace, but Jesus can.

By fulfilling the Scriptures of the prophets, Jesus the Messiah has made it possible for Adam's descendants to live forever with their Creator-King. But not all will live in His kingdom.

 Just as God made His one rule clear to Adam about living in the earthly garden, so God has made His one rule clear to Adam's descendants about living in the heavenly city:

Nothing impure will ever enter it, nor will anyone who does what is shameful or deceitful, but only those whose names are written in the Lamb's book of life (Revelation 21:27).

 The Lamb's book of life is the heavenly registry with the name of every person who, since the time of Adam, has trusted God's way of salvation. The King of glory will not force you or your family to believe in Him and what He has done to rescue you from Satan, sin, death, and hell.

There will be no unwilling subjects in His kingdom. But because the King does not want anyone to perish, He closes His book with an invitation, a warning, and a promise:

"Whoever is thirsty, let him come; and whoever wishes, let him take the free gift of the water of life. I warn everyone who hears the words of the prophecy of this book: If anyone adds anything to them, God will add to him the plagues described in this book.... He who testifies to these things says, 'Yes, I am coming soon.'"

"Amen! Come, Lord Jesus!" (Revelation 22:17-20).

A fter Adam sinned, what did he say to God when God came into the garden calling out to him? Adam shamefully answered,

> "I heard you in the garden, and I was afraid" (Genesis 3:10).

But now, how do some of Adam's descendants react to the Lord's promise to come to earth for them? They joyfully answer,

> "Amen! Come, Lord Jesus!" (Revelation 22:20).

What brought about such transformation? Why are some people no longer afraid to stand before the Judge of the earth? Why are they so excited about seeing the King face to face?

It is because they believe His story and message.

The prophet Isaiah wrote,

> Who has believed our message? … All of us, like sheep, have strayed away. We have left God's paths to follow our own. Yet the LORD laid on him the sins of us all (Isaiah 53:1,6 NLT).

Isaiah summed up the King's story and message in three statements:

1. We have a problem.

> "We have left God's paths to follow our own."

2. God has the solution.

> "The LORD laid on [His Son] the sins of us all."

3. We have a choice.

> "Who has believed our message?"

Do you believe the King?

> We accept man's testimony, but God's testimony is greater because it is the testimony of God, which he has given about his Son. …

> Anyone who does not believe God has made him out to be a liar, because he has not believed the testimony God has given about his Son. And this is the testimony: God has given us eternal life, and this life is in his Son. He who has the Son has life; he who does not have the Son of God does not have life.

> I write these things to you who believe in the name of the Son of God so that you may know that you have eternal life (1 John 5:9-13).

Yes, you can *know*. The King does not keep you guessing.

Have you turned your back on man's religion and believed God's testimony? If so, then you will spend eternity with the King…

> happily ever after.

THE BAD NEWS

As we read at the beginning of His book, the King of the universe created man in His own image and likeness. He made humans for His glory. People would be His special treasure, close friends, and holy citizens in His kingdom of light. But first there must be a time of testing.

The LORD God gave Adam a small test with big consequences. God told him that he was free to eat from all the trees of the garden except one. What did God say would happen to Adam if he broke this one rule?

 Did God tell Adam that he must begin to recite prayers, fast, and do enough good deeds to balance out his bad deeds? *No!* God said, "When you eat of it *you will surely die*" (Genesis 2:17).

We know what happened. Man chose to disobey his Creator-King. Adam and Eve sinned. But did they drop dead that same day? No. So what did God mean when He said, "When you eat of it you will surely die"?

What, according to the Scriptures, is the meaning of death?

 Look at the picture. What is happening with the branch? What will happen to it after it is broken from the tree? Will it be alive? Or dead?

The branch might still look alive, but it will be dead because it has been separated from its source of life.

Death means *separation*. This is bad news.

When Adam and Eve chose to go their own way instead of God's way they lost their connection with God, like a branch cut off the tree. Their relationship with God was dead. They no longer wanted to be with Him. They tried to hide. Adam and Eve were dead spiritually.

Your sins have cut you off from God (Isaiah 59:2 NLT).

 Adam and Eve also began to die physically. Even as the leaves on a broken branch do not dry up instantly, so their bodies did not return to dust the day they sinned. But the aging process had begun. Death was an enemy from which they would not escape.

But the bad news gets worse. Unless God provided rescue, Adam and Eve faced eternal separation from God in "the eternal fire prepared for the devil and his angels" (Matthew 25:41).

Some people mock the idea of hell—a lake of fire where souls contaminated by sin will be quarantined for all eternity. But is it wise to mock what we do not understand? As humans, we cannot grasp the concept of eternity. It is another dimension. People also mocked the prophet Noah as he built the ark and warned them of the coming flood. But once the door of the ark was closed and the flood came, they understood the truth they had mocked. In a similar way, the moment people enter hell, they will understand its solemn logic.

> They will be punished with everlasting destruction and shut out from the presence of the Lord and from the majesty of his power (2 Thessalonians 1:9).

The King will not allow sin to pollute His universe forever.

Sin is the most destructive force and far-reaching disaster on our planet. Sin is the cause of all evil.

Like a contagious disease, Adam's sin has infected us all. Just as each twig and leaf on a broken branch is dead, so each of us is affected by Adam's sin. We are all a part of the Adam branch.

When Adam sinned, sin entered the world. Adam's sin brought death, so death spread to everyone, for everyone sinned (Romans 5:12 NLT).

Back in Moses' day, people had the same wrong idea that people have today. They hoped that if they did more good than bad, God would show them mercy on the Day of Judgment. To correct their wrong thinking, God came down on Mount Sinai in blazing fire and gave the people ten commands to obey. Anyone who did not keep all ten rules perfectly was declared guilty and worthy of death.

The Ten Commandments are like a mirror. If your face is dirty, a mirror helps you see the dirt, but it cannot remove the dirt. In a similar way, the Commandments were not given to make us right with God. Instead, they show us that we are guilty sinners before a holy God. We are unfit to live in His righteous kingdom. We are helpless sinners in need of a perfect Savior.

> For everyone has sinned; we all fall short of God's glorious standard (Romans 3:23 NLT).

The bad news is that we do not measure up to God's perfect standard of goodness. The good news is that there is one person in history who did.

His name is Jesus.

THE GOOD NEWS

The LORD is perfect in justice and mercy. Justice means that the full penalty of the law has been carried out against my sin. Mercy means that the penalty of the law has not been carried out against me.

How could God punish our sin without punishing us?

The answer is found in the Lord Jesus Christ, who came to our rescue.

In Old Testament times, before Jesus came, God set up *the law of the sin offering* to rescue sinners from *the law of sin and death*. God accepted the blood of innocent animals as a payment for sin. This is how He punished sin without punishing the sinner.

But is a lamb a fair trade for a man? No. Animal blood could only picture what justice really required.

What kind of blood could pay off the sin debt of the world? Only the blood of a perfect, infinite Man. The Creator-Word Himself became that Man.

"In the beginning was the Word.... The Word became flesh and made his dwelling among us. We have seen his glory, the glory of the One and Only, who came from the Father, full of grace and truth" (John 1:1,14).

The blood of lambs could only *cover* sin. Jesus is "the Lamb of God, who *takes away* the sin of the world!" (John 1:29).

Remember Abel? God put Abel's sins on the lamb. The lamb was Abel's temporary sin-bearer. Jesus is our permanent Sin-Bearer. God loaded all our sins onto Him.

The lamb that was killed and burned to ashes in Abel's place was a picture of Jesus who paid the full penalty for our sins. That is why, just before He died, Jesus shouted in victory, "It is finished!" (John 19:30).

Justice is satisfied. Mercy is available.

It is this Good News that saves you if you firmly believe it .... Christ died for our sins, just as the Scriptures said. He was buried, and he was raised from the dead on the third day, as the Scriptures said (1 Corinthians 15:2-4 NLT).

T hink of Abraham and his son. Why did God send them to a specific distant mountain for the sacrifice?

God was marking out the place where His own Son would go to die for the sins of the world.

Why did Abraham name the mountain "The LORD will Provide"? Because it was on that mountain that God provided the full and final sacrifice.

What did God provide for Abraham's son? A ram. What has God provided to save you from judgment? Jesus, the Lamb of God.

Do you fear death and judgment? If you put your total trust in Jesus as your Savior, you need not fear, because God has received full payment from Him for your sins and raised Him back to life.

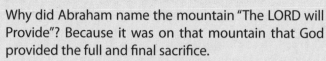

Now think back to Adam and Eve. Their sin and shame made them cover up with fig leaves and want to hide from God. In His justice and mercy, God exposed their sin and clothed them in the skins of sacrificed animals. The shed blood of the animals pictured what was necessary to cover their sin, and the skins of the animals pictured what was necessary to cover their shame.

We all share our ancestors' sin and shame. We fall short of God's righteousness. We are unfit to live with Him. The good news is that on the cross Jesus Christ took our sin and shame. During those hours of darkness, He experienced the separation from God that we deserve. And then He died. But since He had no sin of His own, the tomb could not hold Him.

Because of Jesus' death and resurrection, God offers to cleanse and clothe you: to exchange your sins for His righteousness.

We are all infected and impure with sin. When we display our righteous deeds, they are nothing but filthy rags (Isaiah 64:6 NLT).

I am overwhelmed with joy in the LORD my God! For he has dressed me with the clothing of salvation and draped me in a robe of righteousness (Isaiah 61:10 NLT).

God made him who had no sin to be sin for us, so that in him we might become the righteousness of God (2 Corinthians 5:21).

On Judgment Day, will you stand before God in the rags of your own religious efforts?

Or will you stand robed in the pure righteousness of Christ?

THE MESSAGE IN THE STORY • 4
YOUR RESPONSE TO THE KING

Imagine yourself walking through a lonely forest. Which would you rather meet—a lamb or a lion?

At His first coming, the King of glory was called *The Lamb*. He came in humility to save sinners. When the King returns, He will be called *The Lion*. He will come in majesty to judge unrepentant sinners.

When Jesus comes back, will you rejoice in the presence of your Savior-King or will you tremble before your Judge-King? It all depends on your response to God's message.

When Jesus began to travel and teach, some of His first words were,

"Repent and believe the good news!" (Mark 1:15).

"Repent" means to *change your mind* about what you are trusting in for the right to live in God's kingdom. It means to stop trusting your own way and to start trusting and following God's way.

"Believe the good news" means *to put your faith in the Savior* who died for your sins and rose again to give you new life. But what does it mean to put your faith in someone?

Let me illustrate with a first-hand story from West Africa. It's about two women, Fatu and Bintu.

Both had infections in their eyes. Fatu went to the hospital. The doctor gave her antibiotic eye drops. Her eyes were cured. Bintu went to the traditional healer. He rubbed his "cure" into her eyes. Her eyes turned white and she became blind.

Both Fatu and Bintu had faith. Both women acted on their faith by going to a healer they trusted—but how different the outcome.

When it comes to eternity, everyone trusts in something or someone. Many hang their hope on the religion of their parents. Some side with those who say that life ends at the grave. Others come up with their own ideas about life, death, and eternity. In the end, only one question will matter: Did you choose the truth?

As for me, I've made my choice. I trust the King, who said,

"Everyone on the side of truth listens to me" (John 18:37).

He is the One I want to live with forever. He's the One "who loved me and gave himself for me" (Galatians 2:20).

He is not just *a* king. He's *my* King!

The first man was made to reflect God's image. That image was spoiled by sin. Jesus Christ, "the image of the invisible God" (Colossians 1:15), came to give you new life and to restore God's image in you.

If you have put your faith in Jesus Christ, the King of glory, then, in the eyes of God, you are no longer *in Adam*. You are *in Christ*. You are a favored citizen of heaven and a beloved child of God. You are God's own treasure, which He ransomed with the blood of His own Son.

As a newborn member of God's family you can now call God *Father*. But with great privilege comes great responsibility.

> As obedient children, do not conform to the evil desires you had when you lived in ignorance. But just as he who called you is holy, so be holy in all you do (1 Peter 1:14-15).

As a follower of Christ, you are called to forgive, love, and pray for all people, even your enemies. Jesus says,

> "By this all men will know that you are my disciples, if you love one another" (John 13:35).

As you submit to Him, the Spirit of the Lord Jesus, who came into your heart when you believed the gospel, will help you overcome sin and reflect His holy character.

> The Holy Spirit produces this kind of fruit in our lives: love, joy, peace, patience, kindness, goodness, faithfulness, gentleness, and self-control (Galatians 5:22-23 NLT).

As a child of the King, you have a new purpose in life: to honor Him. You are His ambassador to a lost world. Represent Him well. One day you will see Him face to face, and then you "will be like him" (1 John 3:2). Until then, talk to Him at any time. Praise Him in every situation. Worship and serve Him with others who love Him and His Word. Study the Scriptures daily (start with *Luke*, *John*, *Acts*, and *Romans*). The Holy Spirit is your Teacher. The Bible is your spiritual food and weapon against Satan, who does not want you to think, speak, and act like Jesus. The more you meditate on the Scriptures the stronger you will become spiritually.

I love this word picture from the Psalms:

> As the deer pants for streams of water, so my soul pants for you, O God (Psalm 42:1).

Can you say that?

The choice is yours.

Paul D. Bramsen

resources@rockintl.org

KING OF GLORY
ILLUSTRATED STUDY GUIDE
ENDNOTES

1. You may find ROCK International's book *One God One Message* (by P. D. Bramsen) helpful. It presents the same big picture, but contains four times the information found in *KING OF GLORY*. It provides logical answers to hundreds of questions. Available in print from online booksellers. Available as a free PDF download at **www.king-of-glory.com**

2. Discovered in June of 2014, **ringwoodite** is a bluish, crystal structured rock housed in the Earth's mantle between 525 and 660 km (326 and 410 mi) below the earth's surface. This mantle of ringwoodite reservoir is estimated to contain, in the form of hydroxide, about three times more water than the Earth's oceans combined. This discovery makes it easy to understand the biblical record, which describes the source of the global flood in Genesis 7:11-12: *"On that day all the springs of the great deep burst forth, and the floodgates of the heavens were opened. And rain fell on the earth forty days and forty nights."*

3. Co-published by Emmaus International and ROCK International, ***What if Jesus Meant What He Said?*** (by Nate Bramsen) will challenge you to take Jesus' words seriously. For some other excellent resources to strengthen you in your relationship with the Lord and to encourage you in your study of His Word, check out the Bible study courses (in many languages) and L.I.T. (Life in Truth) discipleship programs at **www.EmmausInternational.com**

4. What follows is an explanation for the **Exodus/Red Sea Crossing/Mount Sinai route** marked on the map on page 150. Scholars hold many different views as to the path by which God led His ancient people away from their slavery in Egypt, *"through the way of the wilderness of the Red sea"* (Exodus 13:18), and *"through the sea on dry ground, with a wall of water on their right and on their left"* (Exodus 14:29), and on to Mount Sinai/Horeb in Arabia. The sea in which God opened a path is called the Red Sea in English and *Yam Suph* in Hebrew (meaning *Sea of Reeds* or *Sea of Seaweed*). The Gulf of Suez and the Gulf of Aqaba are part of this same sea. This ocean body (either as Yam Suph or simply Yam) is referred to about 50 times in the Old Testament.

    One verse that may help identify where God opened the path in the sea is 1 Kings 9:26: *"And king Solomon made a navy of ships in Eziongeber, which is beside Eloth, on the shore of the Red sea (Yam Suph), in the land of Edom."* King Solomon had a fleet of ocean-going ships in what is known today as the Gulf of Aqaba. Geographical and archeological evidence points to that same Gulf (not the Gulf of Suez or some lake) as the place where *"Moses stretched out his hand over the sea, and all that night the LORD drove the sea back with a strong east wind and turned it into dry land"* (Exodus 14:21).

To the east of Aqaba is the region of Midian, where God, 40 years earlier, spoke to the shepherd Moses from a burning bush at *"Horeb the mountain of God"* (Exodus 3:1), promising to bring Moses and the Israelites back to *"this mountain"* after He delivered them from their slavery (Exodus 3:11-12).

As to the site of the Red Sea crossing, on the west side of the Gulf of Aqaba there is a canyon that leads onto Nuweiba Beach (easily seen on satellite maps), a beach large enough to hold the few million people that this nation had become. As Pharaoh's army approached, the Israelites were trapped between the mountains and the sea. Apart from divine intervention they would perish. The wide beach/flood plain of Nuweiba slopes down into the gulf and leads up to the Arabian side. It is the only undersea ridge in the mile-deep gulf of Aqaba. This wide underwater road (unsurprisingly somewhat broken in places) is made up of a hard layer of sand and silt, perfect for walking on once God *"made a way through the sea, a path through the mighty waters"* (Isaiah 43:16). The Scripture tells us that once the people had crossed over, God brought the waters back again and Pharaoh's army of soldiers and chariots were destroyed. To this day, this wide, underwater path is littered with coral formations, many of them still in the shapes of debris such as chariot wheels and shafts. On the Arabian side of the sea in the region of Midian is a mountain with a blackened summit, known as Jabal al-Lawz (Galatians 4:25). It was to this region (Horeb in Midian) that God had promised to bring His chosen people.

Not far from that mountain is a 50-foot high rock, split down the middle with evidence of water erosion, the perfect fit for what is described in Scripture, when the LORD said to Moses, *"'I will stand there before you by the rock at Horeb. Strike the rock, and water will come out of it for the people to drink.' So Moses did this in the sight of the elders of Israel."* And the result was that the LORD *"brought streams out of a rocky crag and made water flow down like rivers"* (Exodus 17:6; Psalm 78:16).

Do your own research. You may want to read the carefully researched 448-page book, *The Exodus Case*, by Swedish medical scientist Dr. Lennart Möller. While some of his deductions may be off, many are irrefutable—rooted in biblical, archeological, and historical data. Also recommended is the objective video *The Exodus Revealed*, by Questar.

Ultimately, we don't need to know where these events took place, we just need to understand that *they did*. The greatest miracle performed in the Old Testament is the Red Sea crossing. The greatest miracle in the New Testament is the resurrection of Jesus Christ. Do we know for sure from which tomb, Jesus rose from the dead? No, but evidence shows that He did rise from the dead on the third day. Don't miss the parallels:

God delivered His people from the angel of death in Egypt because of the blood of the lamb on the door posts (Exodus 12). But what if, after saving them thus, He had not opened a path in the sea? Their deliverance from slavery and death would have been futile.

Now think about Jesus' death and resurrection. As the Lamb of God, He shed His pure and precious blood for us on the cross to save us from God's righteous judgment. But what if He had not risen from the dead? The Scripture (1 Corinthians 15:17,19-20) says: *"If Christ has not been raised, your faith is futile; you are still in your sins. … If only for this life we have hope in Christ, we are of all people most to be pitied.* **But now Christ has been raised from the dead ....**" Indeed He has! (Read the next endnote.)

5   *The evidences for Jesus' resurrection from the dead are numerous and convincing.*

The tomb was empty.

The corpse was nowhere to be found.

The women were the first to witness the empty tomb, hear the angel's announcement, see Jesus alive, touch Him, and speak with Him. If the Gospel records had been invented, do you think the four men who wrote them would have given the women credit for being first in everything?!

The documented post-resurrection appearances of Jesus were many. For decades to follow, hundreds of credible witnesses would testify to having walked and talked with the risen Messiah.

The disciples had seen Jesus suffer and die. They were heartbroken. Their hopes had been dashed because they had the mistaken idea that the Messiah could never die. They had returned to their homes disheartened and afraid. Then something happened. They saw Jesus alive. Suddenly they remembered how Jesus had told them He would be crucified and rise again the third day. At last they understood the words of the prophets.

These former cowards became Christ's bold witnesses.

—From *One God One Message* (P.D. Bramsen), p. 260

Here is what the Holy Spirit inspired the apostle Paul (called "a former terrorist" in Scene 37) to write about God's provision of salvation:
"The message is very close at hand; it is on your lips and in your heart." And that message is the very message about faith that we preach: If you openly declare that Jesus is Lord and believe in your heart that God raised him from the dead, you will be saved. … For [the Scripture says,] "Everyone who calls on the name of the LORD will be saved" (Romans 10:8-9,13 NLT).

Have you believed God's message in your heart?
Have you openly declared that Jesus is LORD?
Have you called on His name?

Open up, ancient gates!
Open up, ancient doors,
and let the King of glory enter.
Who is the King of glory?
The LORD, strong and mighty,
the LORD invincible in battle!
Who is the King of glory?
The LORD Almighty—He is the King of glory!

— PSALM 24 (PROPHET KING DAVID)

CHRONOLOGICAL STORY TOOLS

These big-picture resources are available in many languages.

KING OF GLORY

www.king-of-glory.com

KING OF GLORY **PICTURE BOOK**

With culturally sensitive paintings, this walk through the Bible distills its story and message into 70 scenes.

KING OF GLORY **MOVIE**

This 15-episode, animated visualization of the picture book takes you on an intense, eye-opening journey through the best story ever told.

KING OF GLORY **ILLUSTRATED STUDY GUIDE**

This beautiful 15-lesson companion tool reinforces the truths embedded in the movie and book about God, man, sin, and salvation. Adaptable for all ages and cultures.

KING OF GLORY **COLORING BOOK**

70 chronological pictures for kids of all ages!